Musings
Variant Perspectives

Lapsus Creations

SHIVANI BHANAGAY

I, Shivani Bhanagay, am a budding writer who wishes to bring a positive change in society through words. I am someone who believes in communicating feelings through writing because feelings when written down often touches people's heart.

Welcome to our Society

Welcome to our society, it's a magical place

But be careful, there are thorns pretty much everywhere!

You can do whatever you like, as long as you don't crush any of the thorns in our sight!

You see, Rules are like thorns here, as long as you follow them, you are allowed to roam here and there! "You must be skinny," says the rule because apparently any other body type is considered ugly here! "Your skin should be clear," because marks are not acceptable here!

To sum up, uniqueness doesn't matter here!

You must follow the rule to become a legitimate member of the society, otherwise, they will treat you like hell for the rest of your life!

You must know, we are trying to turn things around here!

We are trying to demolish rules around here!

Pretty soon the new ones will live freely around here,

They will be allowed to be themselves over here!

But for that, we must work now!

because evidently, we are the only ones who can

make a change around here!

Ek tarfa pyar

Bachpan ka woh daur tha,

Jab kudrat nai hame ek dusre sai milaya tha!

Tum ek muskurahat ke sath mujhse milne aaye the,

Dost banogi meri , mujhse puchne ayye the!

Woh "love at first sight " ko mehsoos maine ussi pal kar liya tha!

Woh 10 saal ki ladki nai pehli bar pyar ki massomiyat ko mehsoos kiya tha!

Kai bar lagta tha ki tumne dil ki baatein bata du,

Par shayad hamari dosti ko khone ka dar mere mann mai kahi samma sa gaya tha!

Tumhe kissi aur ke sath dekhkar dil udaas sa ho jata tha,

Kai baar toh dil ko sambhalna mushkil sa ho jata tha!

Par phir tumhare chehre par woh muskurahat dekhkar dil apne aap sambhal jata tha!

Ek tarfa pyar ke taakat ka andaza mujhe uss pal ho chuka tha!

Stay strong

Hey you,

I know you are feeling blue,

But hang in there, you will feel better soon!

You might feel like the darkness has consumed you, but my friend there is light,

You just need to open your eyes.

I know how difficult it is to smile when your heart just denies you to have that joy,

I know how difficult it is to talk when words refuse to come out of your mouth...

My friend,

It's okay to rest for a while,

It's okay to ask someone for their advice

It's okay to ask for help,

But it's not okay to punish yourself in order to feel alive! I know it's difficult,

but please fight for a while...

You will thank yourself for the rest of your life!

Gender Norms!

When I hear them say, boys, don't cry,

I wanted to ask them how pathetic are they from the inside?

When they say girls should be quite,

I wish to educate them from the highest pitch of my voice!

"Boys don't wear pink" this is what they say!

I want to tell them to please mind their own business.

They say girls should dress decently,

I wanted to ask them to open their mind a little bit

Men should be masculine, I heard them say,

I wish to laugh at their ridiculous thought process

They say girls aren't funny,

I want to use my sarcasm to mock them frequently

For ages, they have been saying

Men are the head and women are the supporter

I want to ask,

How long are we going to agree to this bullshit?

Is this how it will be?

Are we going to normalize these gender norms and gender inequality?

Or are we going to wake up and finally do something about it?

ANTARA

I'm twenty-five and I love to write rhymes some-times. On weekdays I'm a technical copywriter. In between, I'm writing sad poetry while watching Schitt's Creek. Winter is my favourite season and you can always find me lounging in the afternoon sun when I can, with a book and some sun-tan. Riding out the apocalypse with my family in Allahabad.

Fear of Being Unkind

I keep thinking about right and wrong
Wondering if I'm being good and just and fair
While brushing my teeth
Folding clothes
Feeding the hungry
Dressing up wounds
Wounds of people I tolerate and love and care
My tongue curling around the ghost of cruel
words, about to exhale frustrations
Sometimes I stop, most times I don't
Then negotiate to compensate
By being nice and kind and selfless
While brushing off insults
Folding my temper
Feeding their egos
Dressing up wounds
At sundown, in silent corners.
Wounds of my own.

Dying Embers

Can you hear them? Hear them fight,
Licking around the urn, holding on tight.
Crackling away, the flames amber;
On a night cold and somber.

The swell of winter blowing,
The dying Embers still glowing
Soldiers of the night
Blazing with all their might.

Like a whiplash the rain pelts
Where it lands, making welts
Oh! but the callous cold
The Embers intrepid and bold

Far away in a bleak village somewhere
The tramp rests cold, no shroud to share
From this world, there's none to call
For the next, the Embers be her pall

A waif weeps, alone on the roads
The ruthless chill that goads
Why then, the happy crackle mesmerizes
It warms and soothes the aching cries

Can you hear them? Hear them fight,
Licking around the urn, holding on tight.
Slipping away, like grains of sand
Giving their all, salving the land

The swell of winter surmounts
The dying Embers renounce
Selfless soldiers of the night
Blazing no more- no sound, no sight.

A Call to Myself

In passing sometimes
when I look in your eyes
I understand
the meanings of phrases
I left marked
in age-yellowed pages
And then you see me
once or twice
on your own, you believe me
and want to love me

I am not of faith
swimming in the sea
of believers
I'm fighting the current
But you know it's easier to stop.
So I fight harder
to break the mould
'If you flaff around in the water too long
you will grow old'
When have I ever done what I'm told?
And in all the chaos
you're my only hold.

I let you trace
the moles on my face
that you hate so much
you remind me every day
with your imperfect lips
that are stained.
I want to kiss you

Kiss me as you do
All my dreams
centre around you
Loving you is painful
You are beautiful
and I've been cruel.

Now it's us!
Riding on our blasphemy
into the shores of the
pious liars
hoping for life
and knowing
this futile naivete
will puncture
the moment we crash
on the red sands;
colours of the con-man.
Let me make love to you
before the voices quiet
before we lose sight
I want to see you see me
The call of Oblivion was the tether to our sanity
I hope it's the silence that awaits
I am not of faith
and you are with me.

Better Friends

But if we had been friends
I perhaps would have treasured you more
For after the passion haze ends
And our limbs tangled, lips welded

Remain no more
Only the eyes will blaze
With discovered hate
As the heart mourns the loss
Sitting by the ashes
Of a happier past.
So be my friend, my lover!
We'll find many to share the bed
I don't want to detest
What is already dead
You know what I know
We have always been better friends.

Anxiety is My Clingy Lover

In a dance-off
with the mirror
waiting
to see
who breaks;
unmoving
I try
to keep pace
I'm struggling
in a giant
masquerade
where I'm the only one
with a mask
on my face

ISHWA RAVAL

I am from Gandhinagar. I am 17 years old and I have been writing poetry since I was 15 years old. I am still a student, studying in 12th. I have grown in a joint family. I had always an aspiration of being a writer but never thought it would be too soon.

Poetry 1:

I never need to compare my self with others because there was always my mother
I never need to be bold because there was always my mother tender to hold me
I never need anyone's hug because my mother's body is a touch of heal
I never need to be sad for my Marks because my mother was glad for my task
I never need to be in dilapidated avert because my mother was always alert
I never need a group for unity because my mother was enough as a unit
I never need to love mustard because my mother always make the sweet custard
I never need anyone ever because my mother is with and for me forever.

Poetry 2:

The world stands around us
They want us, as they did
They are coins
They flip as they wish
The world manipulate us as they wish

The world speaks about us
They won't talk, as they did
They are gossipers
They herald as they wish
The world rejects us as they wish

The world asks from us
They want more, as they did
They are beggars
They spend as they wish
The world dilapidated us as they wish

The world takes from us
They want servant, as they did
They are cheaters
They reprimand as they wish
The world hates us as they wish

The world shows us
They want attention, as they did

They are lacquer
They pretend as they wish
The world deflect us as they wish

The world gives up on us
They want more, as they did
They are killers
They hurt as they wish
The world finishes us as they wish...

Poetry 3:

My mother wants to cry with joy
She is waiting for time
When I stand up on stage
And crowd claps for me

My mother wants to dance with tears
She is waiting for me
When I do with my own deed
And world salutes for me

My mother wants to hurt with heal
She waiting for destiny
When I start my journey
And finish it for me

My mother wants to grow with cut
She is waiting for miniatures
When I sprout with happiness
And people respect me.

Poetry 4:

Stolen pulse in a lying heart.....
Broken heartbeat in a damaged chest...
Fake being in an awful human...
Wasted tears in a cried eye...
Horrible pain in a burning skin...
Disgusted talk in a tilted face...
Faded memories in a disable mind...
Rough time in an aged watch...
Suffered feelings in an anxiety body...
The different manner in a similar situation...
Colourless motion in a dark soul...
Rapid pace in an unstable life...
The changed person in the same street...
Nightmare fear came true in a real existence world...

Poetry 5:

रब से क्या मांगे तुम्हें
 मांगा था तुमसे तुम्हें
 तुम्हारी बेवफाई भी नजरअंदाज की
 तुम ही ना छोड़े
 छोड़े आंखों में आंसू
 वह आंसू भी हम पी गए
 फिर पिलाया प्यार का नशा
 नशे में भूल गए कि यह तो झूठ है
 होना तो वही होगा जो होता आया है
 तुम्हारी बेवफाई .....और हमारी खुदाई ......सिर्फ तुमसे..

SHARADA WALI

So here are just a few unspoken words by an amateur teen-aged writer.

You will find a few of these write-ups much relatable as they completely inspired me from my real-life situations, for example, the upcoming 'chahtein', 'lamhe', 'yaadein', a few motivational ones as well as the ones based on relationships - from this piece of work.

Inspirational Unspoken Words...

Kyo hai apni in haath ki lakeero par nirbhar
Jab tayy kar sakta hai tu apni zindagi ka har safar
Chod de wo gam saare jo tabah kar deti hai teri
himmat
Aur kar dikha hasil har khwaab ko bhale hi saath
na de teri qismat.

Chal zindagi,ek nayi shuruat karte hai.
Kal jo umeedein auro se ki thi ,wo aaj khud se karte
hai.

Samajh na beith apne aap ko tu ek aam tara
Bheedh me bhi to chamak raha hai tu maano ek
khoobsurat sitara

Chahtein...

Bas yahi chahat hai,
Ek aazad panchi ki tarah udna chahti hu,
Har us khwaab ko pura karna chahti hu jo maine
apne khuuli aankho se dekhe hai,
Bas ek aam zindagi hi to jeena chahti hu auro ki
tarah,
Kya itna mushkil hota hai ek ladki ko uski
chahtein pura karne ki aazadi dena?

Lamhe...

Har us lamhe ko jeena chahti hu,

Jab mera dil tumhe dekh kar muskurata,
Jab tumhari khushi me hi mera dil bhi khush ho
jata,
Jab tumhe dukhi dekh mera dil bhi rooth jata,
Har us pal ko dobara jeena chahti hu,
Tumhare saath, sirf tumhare saath..

Kyo farak padta hai?
Kya farak padta hai?
rang kala hai ya gora,
Dharm hindu hai ya musalmaan,
Ye to upar waala hi tayy karta hai ke
Insaan accha hai ya bura,
To sawal hona chahiye,
Farak kyon padta hai?

Yaadein..

Kuch meethi si,
Kuch khatti si,
Kuch hamare dil ko khush kar jaati hai,
Kuch ussi dil ko thes pohcha deti hai,
Lekin woh yaadein hi to hoti hai jo ek adhuri zind-
agi ko pura karti hai...

Rishtein...

Jis rishte ki tulna mai chaand ki khoobsurati se kar
rahi thi
Ussi rishte ne yaad dila diya ke chaand par daag
bhi hote hai

Ye hai ek khoobsurat kahani do lafzo mai kaise
bayan karu
Do dilon ka hai ye atoot rishta ise mai kaise vyakt
karu

Kyo us rishte ke khone se dukhi hai jo kabhi tha hi
nahi
Agar waade sacche hote to dukh ek tarfa nahi hota

Na chahkar bhi paraye ban jaoge
Na hokar bhi galat samjhe jaoge
Bas koi na samajhne wala apna hona chahiye

PRIYANKA CHAVAN

Namaste, My name is Priyanka Chavan (Pri). I am a proper Mumbaikar who enjoys street vada pav and tapri wali chai more than McD's burger and CCD's coffee. Well, by profession I am an IT engineer, but by passion, I am a heartful writer. I had started writing poetries when I was in 7th std. All thanks to my teacher who inspired me to write after listening to my different perspectives about things. That time I wrote almost 4-5 poetries till 8th std. After that, my teacher got transferred and my inspiration went with her. Then I got busy in studies and board exams. And then after 10th, I opt science field because the one who gets 90% or more than that marks, they should opt science this is was what society use to say. And then the biggest adventure came into my life. That was my Btech degree. And after doing all the struggle for 4 years, I felt like something is missing in life. Something which makes me feel happy, relaxed, the thing which gives me inner peace. So, there I again start writing. Till now, I have written almost 100 poetries, shayaris and stories. I have also represented some of them in open mic shows too. So, this is all about me till now. I have given some of my poetries below, so you will get to know about my writing a bit. And if you want to go for a trip on my dreamy land of words, then you can connect with me on Instagram and Youtube.

Instagram : @priyankachavan17

@pri.ke.lafz

Youtube : Pri ke Lafz

Poetry 1 : Zindagi ka woh mod hi aisa tha..

Jab woh bolte the tab hum chupchap sunte the
Jab hum bolte the tab woh chupchap sunte the
Batein kam aur sunna sunana jyada ho gaya tha
Zindagi ka woh mod hi kuch aisa aaya tha

Pehle hamari khamoshi bhi khud se jaan lete the
hamare bina kuch kahe hi sab samaj jate the
ab khamoshiya itni bad gayi thi ki ishq hi kha-
mosh ho gaya tha
Zindagi ka woh mod hi kuch aisa aaya tha

Pehle hamare hath se banaye hue khane ki badi
tarife karte the
Khana khane ke baad bhi bar bar ungliyan chatate
rehte the
Ab har niwala khane ke sath sath taana aane lag
gaya tha
Zindagi ka woh mod hi kuch aisa aaya tha
Shaadi ke pehle humse mile bina unka din nhi jata
tha
Humse pure din baat na huyi to dil bechain sa ho
jata tha
Aaj samne hokar bhi sath na hone jaisa lagne lag
gaya tha
Zindagi ka woh mod hi kuch aisa aaya tha
Pehle hamare har ek jajbaat ki kimat woh bak-
hoobi jante the
Itni mohabbat thi ki nafrat to hum bhul hi gaye
the

Aaj hamare jakhmo ka dard bhi unhe janna na tha
Zindagi ka woh mod hi kuch aisa aaya tha

Poetry 2 : Maine Dekhi Huyi Mardangi

Aaj fir maine mard ko apni khawaisho ka gala gho-
tate dekha hai..
Aaj fir use zimmedariyon ke bojh ke tale dabte
dekha hai..

Khud ko bhuka rakh kar hamesha dusro ka pet
bharte dekha hai..
Apne liye wahi fate purane kapde apno ke liye
kharidte dekha hai..

Kisi apne ke juda hone par use tootate bikharte
bhi dekha hai..
Duniya ke samne kathor man par akele me rote
dekha hai..

Paiso ki parwah na kar hamesha dusro ke liye so-
chte dekha hai..

Khud ki jaan jokhim me dal kar apno ke liye mar
mitate dekha hai..

Apna dard chupakar dusro ka dard kam karte
dekha hai..
Dusro ko koi takleef na ho bas usi ka dhyan rakhte
dekha hai..

Apne hisse ki khushi bhi hamesha dusro me
baatate dekha hai..

Saari pareshani magar khud akele hi jhelna seekha
hai..

Aaj fir maine mard ko kisi ka beta, pati, baap, bhai
bante dekha hai..
Aaj fir maine inn haiwano ki duniya me insaan
roop bhagwan dekha hai..

Poetry 3 : Kismat hi footi hai

Ye zindagi bhi humse iss kadar roothi hai..
Kya kare janab hamari to kismat hi footi hai..

Log kehte hai pyaar ek jail booti hai..
Unhe kya pata jab hamari kismat hi footi hai..

Humne bhi uss pe poori mohabbat looti hai..
Lekin ishq ke mamle me to kismat hi footi hai..

Uske wapas aane ki ab ummeed bhi tooti hai..
Dua bhi kuch kr na saki kismat jo footi hai..
Ishq ke gam me zindagi aisi ghooti hai..
Dawa bhi kis kaam ki jab kismat hi footi hai..

Uske dur jaane se kitni khwaishe chuti hai..
Rab bhi kya kare jab kismat hi footi hai..

Sabko lagta hai hamari dasata hi jhooti hai..
Unhe bhi kya kahe jab ki kismat hi footi hai..

Ab bas bichdo ko milane me hi zindagi jooti hai..
Ta ki log na kahe unki bhi kismat footi hai..

Poetry 4 : Woh tapri wali chai

Café ki coffee se hum aaj bhi woh tapri wali chai
peena pasand karte hai..
Maaf karna janab hum aaj bhi woh old vali zindagi
jeena pasand karte hai..

Ye digital likhavat se hum aaj bhi wo shahi kalam
se likhe huye khat pasand karte hai..
Hume maaf karna janab hum thode purane kisam
ke hai..

Ye e-books se hum aaj bhi kitabo ki khushbu sung-
hkar padhna pasand karte hai..
Maaf karna janab hum aaj bhi woh old vali zindagi
jeena pasand karte hai..

Ye rap remix ke generation me hum aaj bhi lata rafi
ji ke geet sunna pasand karte hai..
Hume maaf karna janab hum thode purane kisam
ke hai..
Aaj ki ye online relationship se hum woh 7 janm ke
kasme vaade karna pasand hai..
Maaf karna janab hum aaj bhi woh old vali zindagi
jeena pasand karte hai..

Uss social media vali chats se hum aaj bhi sath
baithkar gapshap ladana pasand hai..
Hume maaf karna janab hum thode purane kisam

ke hai..

Iss 21st century ki artificial duniya me aaj bhi kuch original paane ki koshish karte hai..
Kyun ki hum aaj bhi zindagi se juda nhi to zindagi se jude rehna pasand karte hai..

And, if you are already here, it means you have already booked the ticket to my dreamy land. Pri, welcome you all. And, thanks for staying till the end.

RUTHU KARAT

Hey, I am Ruthu Karat and poetry has always been the Aspirin to my soul.

The subtle effect of calmness, the feel of healing and the hope that comes along with poetry is tremendous! It's like the whispers lost in the air, your words lost in your paper... And these are a few of my words...

Dedicated to my Rum Rum...thank you for being my best friend and my constant!

Ruthu Karat is a fourteen-year-old girl, born and brought up in the business centre of Kerala, Kochi, the Queen of the Arabian Sea. She resides with her parents and an elder sister. Being a voracious reader, she is inspired and enthralled by how much the universe of books can change and constantly accompany a person.

She is herself a humanist who believes in rights and equality to every human being. Apart from writing, she is a music fiend and loves spending time with her friends and family.

Instagram - @ruthukarat

The poet inside me...

She comes alive

when she's in the dark

Lets out her despair,

with some words

Let poetry form in the paper

just as the tear in her eye

She doesn't talk yet holds

the pen upright

And still, it's unreasonable to other

for what she does

And the darkest of times

brings alive

The poet inside me.

Your love

On a dreamy rainy night

I dreamt once again about you.

Among the fairy lights

I thought about our times.

You gave me an escape from reality and sins

All I wanted was your hazel gaze

and more of you to hold through the night.

We drifted apart not so soon,

After cupid passed us by

Butterflies still reside in my stomach

But in a spell asleep; that breaks

Only by your kiss.

Devdas

Don't give me that Devdas look, she said

Telling that this was our 'end'

'You'll never learn' she said before,

she left me hanging on my own

I did no harm, but she wanted to 'let go'

of everything we had, so we did right,

In life, in the world of our own.

Friends said to try tinder, but that wasn't my show

'Devdas' they teased, but none of them knew,

That my tears too had a story to tell of their own.

I smiled and let go of her,

But not my love for her;

As I promised her my heart,

just as her own.

Sometimes

Your touch was enough to
wake me anew,
Your scent was crucial to my soul
Love hurts, but it's still worth the pain if it's for
you.
Love is corrupt, love is selfish
But for your love,
Oh how I'd rob the globe and the celestial bodies,
Only to lay them at your divine feet.

Aura

The aura around you my love,
Indescribable as it can be
Got me fascinated and enthralled
Knowing that you are mine.
What are you?
I quite often retire to my thoughts running
But still, I do not desire to ever know
For maybe you are a dream,
I never want to rouse away from.

Her love

Laying on my bed,

with the thoughts just of her.

Knowing that it's the end

How hard can it go?

Her scent is fading and her face just a blur now

Her love was a rose but with sharp thorns,

that pierced through my heart,

leaving me bleeding on my own.

Our memories haunt me, never like they did before.

I mask a smile through this time

But when I'm all alone, tears flood my eyes just as I
let go

I wish we had tomorrow,

just so we could stay forevermore.

KIMAYA RANAWADE

My name is Kimaya Ranawade and I am born and brought up in Pune itself.

As few people know the meaning of Kimaya, it means magic. I want people to believe in magic. Trying to make people feel the magic in poems.

A poet, a writer, currently pursuing MBA in media and communication.

Gravity

Have I ever mentioned this to you?

You always have all of my attention and in your absence you have my thoughts occupied.

All my interests lie in this one paradise with you.

And you know it's not just a fling but a song that won't end until we die.

You love me and I love you, a love so strong just for us two.

It's your smile that gets me through.

Your charming ways, the tender things you say and the kisses I insist.

Afterall those incomplete days and nights we go through, every day when I see you,

It's you I love, it's you I adore.

Each time your eyes look into mine, I am help-lessly in heaven.

Only you can lit my spark with just a simple touch!

 You're my sun that shines brightly throughout my entire day.

You're my stars that keep me safe from darkness.

You always have all of my attention and in your absence you have my thoughts occupied.

You're the gravity that holds me down in every way.

Rising Elegy

The pain of being without you is too much to bear sometimes.

Missing you is getting harder and it simply feels like a crime.

Our love had lightening and its full of Venus luck.

But love is like a tyrant as it devours the heart completely and sucks.

I am afraid, the heart is a trifle when love possesses.

Now I see how far I have fallen for you and it's not less.

I need you but you aren't here.

I don't want to get used to this, that's why I fear.

We have this distance and honestly, I am halfway to frail.

I think I just need a cocktail!

Why would I ever want our love to decay??

At night, I get so lonely and everything just turns grey.

Maybe I am overthinking and having a missing you syndrome.

But darling, I'll always wait for you, till you come home.

Butterflies with broken wings

In this forest, the trees are darker, the ocean is deeper.

Where I cry all night long

Tears in the heart, do not reach the eyes.

And tears freeze into ice.

Beyond the streets of heartbreaks, tears and sadness.

Emptiness is a whole new world.

While I feel two emotions combined.

In love with you,

Yet not.

I have no name for this feeling,

Where our almost will always haunt me.

You fell in love with a frozen heart.

So when spring arrived, you didn't know what to do.

Scars don't hurt unless you can forget how they once did.

Once I held this forest so strong,

And now,

I am just another butterfly with broken wings and a handful of dreams.

Winter warmth

In the midst of an ordinary day, flashbacks of him are all I remember.

I want to wrap them up in linen and place them in an old cigar box,

I'd tuck it away.

Safely in the top drawer of my bedside table,

So he would know I'll never let those pieces of him go.

Somewhere between hello and goodbye

There was love,

So much of love.

He had this amusing spark in his eyes, to conquer anything in the world I would ask for.

His hands were peace to hold in, as the warmth will pass on and radiate my soul.

On the coldest nights, I'll look for his glow.

That still ignites my mind and lits up my heart.

DR MRUNMAI NILJIKAR

I am 25 and I am not a practising dentist. Much more interested in words, I prefer to indulge myself in books and words.

There was a time, people would call me a social butterfly. Little did they know, the butterfly prefers warm sips of coffee, a cosy nook and a magnanimous pile of books.

I was 14 when I penned down my first poem. It was about 'letting go'. Now that I think of it, I wonder what a 14-year-old odd teenager wanted to let go of.

I don't think I ever wanted anyone to like what I wrote, it was and it still is something highly personal to me. It's sheer happiness to read your own words, a week or a month or a year later and feel the exact surge of emotions I did when I actually wrote it.

Poetry is the only way I know to express my usually suppressed emotions.

MONSOON REMINDS ME OF YOU...

Feeling your icy fingertips,
as they glide down my neck
I sense your gaze
as the moon leads in a haze.
The fall that follows
brings about changes
your favourite maple thus mellows.

As dark and cold winter dwindles into Spring,
your rosy lips beam.
When your gleefully vibrant eyes meet mine
I witness the warm summer,
where all you do, is shine
I see you,
dripping in mango juice
that trickles down your mouth.
wholesomeness so delightful,
my intentions uncouth.

Just as I crave,
Pitter-patter drops topple on my face.
like your kisses, they linger on my nape.
wet soil soothes me,
just as I feel your embrace
Because Monsoon,
as it comes
validates your absence
triggers my senses and irks my defences.
because Monsoon
as it comes,

always reminds me of your lost presence.

SONG OF LOVE? or BIRCHES OF ESCAPE?

You paint a pretty picture,
Like the glimmer of lilac,
Across our dull pink sky.
The passerines, flying high;
The kites, higher.
Little birds that spot berries atop.
I see them now.

I want to sit with you,
Amidst the Birch trees,
On the archaic wooden bench,
That grins on our backs;
While we sing, The song of love.
LOVE,
that is different,
the one that gives courage.
COURAGE,
to escape the pansies of this world,
to walk tall,
like theses birches in the Garden of our Love.
Let us take a stroll,
You and I, walk with the woodland,
Till the sundowns in gold.

Come back later,
To the moonless sky,
where the stars shine and

so do our eyes;
where the bareness of the bench,
Concealed;
But that of our hearts,
Revealed...

LILY IN MY GARDEN:

Rare are occasions when the heart melts,
the deceptive element ends,
and the distance between us is more than just a
drag of miles.

Things that were left unsaid,
Feelings that were untold,
And memories that couldn't be formed.

My mind ponders
whether it was meant to be;
For you to get to know me.
Or was it meant to be,
For my repressed heart,
To open up and fly,
To invite you to peep,
In the deepest nooks
Of my broken heart.

Rare are occasions when the mind settles,
With just a stir of cheer,
That these dragged miles,
Can be flown in and out.
That,
Things will be said,

Feelings shared,
And a lifetime of memories,
Waiting to be formed.

Like the Lily in my garden,
I live every day,
I don't even care that the day might end.
Because the Lily in my garden,
Tells me every day...
" Fight for life, fight for love, and fight for every person,
Who you know,
Is just right"

THE PRODIGAL OBSERVANT

That day, the earth was drenched.
The gloomy sky,
Dripped drops of purity,
The water, untainted
Nuzzled my face calmly.

Wondering what this feeling evokes,
I peered at the world,
That stretched above me,
Like a trampoline,
my heart spread its wings
The horizon was unseen,
The sun lost in the tumult.

My eyes soared and explored,
Only to be mesmerized,
By the magnificent play...

Of colours that glided,
The world above was shielded,
With vibrance of love,
With a sense of empathy,
That challenges the perception of man.
A pair of birds that flew,
Brought me back,
The rapidly firing neurons,

were now conscious of the land.
The Prodigal observant knew,
what the world beneath lacked!

NAMEERA SALLUM

Nameera Sallum is a poetess and a writer from the city of biryani. Most of her work is about love, life lessons, and social issues. She writes in English, Hindi and Urdu. As a tri-lingual writer, Nameera believes that writing soothes her soul. Her work has appeared in Maples, Reverie, Je T'aime and more.

Email - nameerasallum@gmail.com

Instagram handle - @nameera_sallum

NAME

They met at an event.
He had already fallen for her.
She observed him throughout the event.
And he knew about it.
The next day she got a text from him.
They began to talk.
As time passed by, they became best friends.
He never confessed.
She could sense his feelings for her.
They had become very important for each other.
They prioritized things accordingly and were equally ambitious.
Both of them knew but never confessed.
They used to talk about helping each other in finding their respective soulmates.
Yet never confessed.
He was scared of losing their friendship.
Whereas she didn't want to mess up things for both of them.
After a year or so they got occupied with their settlement and barely spoke.
And now when they think of giving it a name,
What will they call it?
Was it just for time being?
Did they not know that it would end someday?
Can it be called true friendship as both of them tried not to mess up?
Can it be called love as they were so into each

other?
Or
Is it not necessary to give it a name at all?

ONLINE STRANGERS

This is a story of two people who met online.

The guy was a shy person and also an introvert.

Whereas, the girl was opposite to him.

They had few things in common,

Which made them become good friends.

They started dating after a while.

They lived in different cities and never met.

Although the distance isn't a factor that could ruin love,

Somehow, their friendship started to fade.

And the love spark was absent too.

As time passed, they started getting into silly fights.

They blamed each other for not being there when it was necessary.

Eventually, time made them realize a few things,

That they had a healthy relation as friends and were not meant to be lovers.

It took a while for them to figure out things mutually.

In the end, they got separated and decided to remain friends.

They respected the decision.

The good thing about being friends was,

They started to share many things and were much closer than before.

Now, they have got their different life partners.

On an important note,

They are happy!

SOME PEOPLE IN OUR LIFE ARE JUST MEANT TO BE FRIENDS.

NOTHING MORE OR NOTHING LESS.

LOVE

They barely knew each other,

He decided to invite her to his birthday-outing.

They had a mutual friend for their company.

Everything went well.

They started texting and knowing each other furthermore.

There weren't any signs or intentions of love among them.

Eventually, they became best friends.

Nothing could separate them.

But he had already fallen for her.

He wasn't sure about how she felt for him.

Like all others, he did not want to ruin their friendship by confessing.

Someday, he realized that he couldn't carry so many emotions all alone.

Trusting their friendship and his intuition, he confessed!

To his surprise, she said yes!

On the other hand, both were worried about the friendship being ruined.

At that moment, they promised to remain best friends' as well.

And, it worked!

They made the best couple ever in the town.

Little did they know that they had broken the stereotypes.

The "lovers can never be best friends" myth was proved to be a myth indeed!

They were in love.

But, the friendship of best friends in them remained alive.

FORGIVE

You broke the promises.

You broke the trust between us.

You broke my heart.

You broke us.

I know how sorry you are.

But it's too late.

It is not about being late or early in seeking forgiveness.

It depends on the impact it had on me.

It depends on the effectiveness of our emotions.

I had never given a thought to forgive you.

I think I never will.

I cannot let you destroy me anymore.

NOT HAPPENING!

NEHA SETH

Hello readers,

I'm Neha Seth aka "Avika', from Varanasi. Currently, pursuing Bachelors in Management Studies from Mumbai University. I started writing when

I was in 5th standard & my first poem was dedicated to my mentors who have always guided me through the way. For me, writing is peace. My pen has listened to me more than anybody could ever do. Just because I write doesn't mean that I'm so much into reading, not at all. But yes I've read certain books & out of those books "The Dark between Stars" by Atticus, is one of my favourite. I love reading poetry collections.

Apart from writing I also like travelling because I believe that I wasn't born to be just in one corner of the world, but to wander with my thoughts around the world. I think everyone can write & for that you just need to match "the right word with the right feeling & there the pen flows". Have a happy reading ahead.!

Thank you so much!

Dear Mirror,

I know if everybody denies to identify me, you would do.
If I lose myself in this journey you would not leave me.
When everybody leaves, you will hold on to me.
So dear mirror I know you have a glimpse of my soul.
Even if I don't owe a corner in anyone's heart, you keep me closer to yourself.
You do it, right?

-Neha

EFFORTS

We put into the threads

of relations

with the pearls of care,

all our flesh & sweat

moreover our blood & bones

seeking a heart full of emotions,

asking for a forever to be

because you know nothing comes for free.

-Neha

YOUNG YEARS

As time passes by

Stomach filled with butterflies

Living the young years of life

Aiming to board the flight

The world I see is ready to welcome

With its arms open

No worries & no troubles

Only to play the songs on shuffle

A friend opening beer of bottle

& I get the truffle.

-Neha

Varanasi

Reet bhi hai,

Aur preet bhi,

Jeevan bhi hai,

Aur maut bhi yahin,

Shiv bhi yahin,

Aur shakti bhi yahin.

Hai sab kuch yahin pe

Aur kuch bhi nahi.

-Neha

VARSHA ROHRA

Varsha Rohra is a speech and drama trainer and a coding instructor. She is the founder of Vocalize- an institute that aims at enhancing the communication skills among children and adults. An engineer by qualification who after working for 2 years in a software company decided to quit without any plan B. She believes that teaching happened to her and her sheer love for kids makes her respect the profession more.

A lover of words and poetry she began teaching speech and drama and fell in love with the intricacies of performing on stage. Her love for arts, poems, and short stories encourages her to continue writing and performing on stage. She will immediately befriend you if you quote Rumi. Her favourite place to be is the window seat on an aeroplane because she always prefers her head to remain in the clouds. She survives on a generous dose of caffeine and loves the vibe of cosy cafes. She truly believes a lot can happen over coffee!

Insta id- varshascribbles_

1.Uncomfortable

I was once told that

There always are two types of fears

Good fear and bad fear

Good fear compels you to do things properly

So that you don't feel guilty

So that you have the accomplishment to be proud of

Good fear is extremely necessary

Bad fear, however, is something that makes you so nervous you just don't begin working

Out of sheer nervousness out of the fact that it will make you uncomfortable

The thought of us being uncomfortable haunts us

Throughout our life, we try to find our own comfort zone

Be it with the people we meet, the subjects we learn, the jobs we take-up

I remember growing up all of us cousins were in the same school

And I was so comfortable with them I barely had other friends

I was shy, timid, uncomfortable

To open up to speak to mingle around

I would watch TV because that made me comfortable

I would diss math all the time and I never prac-
tised any of it

I was certain that no matter how hard I try I could
never get the correct answer

I ate rice, a lot of it. Because that brought comfort

But life had its own set of surprises planned

I took up Engineering that had a lot of math

I reduced eating rice because given my size it was
wise!

I completely stopped watching TV

And started attending open mics and concerts instead

And all these changes which I never explored out
of sheer discomfort

Became the only sources of comfort

But the only thing that is super grateful for exploring

Is the people.

I started talking to all the people without feeling
uncomfortable

I now knew that people were really kind

And a single person or a bunch of people won't always comfort you

I found comfort in people who weren't like me

Comfort in people who disagreed yet listened to
me

Comfort in people who were absolute strangers

but entered my life in the form of angels

The reluctant and scared me who never even smiled at people

Started narrating stories and hitchhiking carefree!

I found utmost comfort in what I felt was really uncomfortable

There always was a fear in me

There always will be some fear in me

I guess that's a part of me

But it no longer makes me feel bad, it no longer makes me feel uncomfortable

2.You don't weigh the pain

On a scale of 1-10, how much does it hurt?
She asked me
And I had no answer to it
I had never weighed my pain
For the sake of answering, I said 6
Because you see that's safe, neither too less nor too high
Being mediocre has always been a safe choice
That's why when people ask you how you're doing
The usual answer is "am fine"
You don't often say am extremely happy or am extremely sad.
But honestly, you are too happy or too sad most of the times
However, we're never taught to accept and ex-

press it.
So you bottled it in an airtight container
Gulped down the tablet without any water and told you're fine
You were never taught to unhesitatingly let them know you just cried
You were never explained the importance of knowing you are not fine
Because the moment you felt something was wrong
You reminded yourself
That it wasn't that bad.
You thought of people who go through much worse.
You thought of people battling their way out.
People smiling, people shining... And considered that though you feel rotten right now.
The pain will go away somehow.
So you suppressed it again...Didn't let it breathe.
What you thought as 6 was actually 9
And because you never let it out you silently raised it to ten
The next time you are asked
On a scale of 1-10
How much does it hurt?
Acknowledge the fact that it does hurt. It hurts a lot.
The pain that you experience is not the same as theirs.
The way you fight is not the same as they do.
But in no way does it mean
Their pain is more and yours is less.
Pain is something you never weigh.

If at any time you feel.
You are going through the excruciating amount of pain
Don't fake a smile and believe you've kissed it goodbye
Make room for it, nurture it, and whenever you feel comfortable to kick it goodbye

3.Sticky Notes
A haiku is a specific type of Japanese poem
It has a total of seventeen syllables
Divided into three lines of 5,7,5 syllables
I love reading a haiku
It brings a wide smile on your face
When little lines leave a huge impact
I love reading little lines
Small stanzas
Verses that aren't very long
Even if they aren't written by prominent poets and renowned writers
Lines that weren't really meant for reading by a lot of people
Like the not so big bucket lists
And the tiny to-do lists
You write it for yourself and read yourself
But they give you a sense of satisfaction
A desire to dream
A happy hope
I'd like to read your bucket list and to-do lists
But make sure they aren't too big
I love reading scribbles and compliments
Oh! I crave for compliments

A lot of them!
And I guess all of us do
So, I try to give as much as I can
People need to be told they are precious
Places need to be told they are loved
I have a habit of reading what's written on colour-
ful papers
Small squares bright in colour with very little
glue just enough to stick on surfaces
You usually find them in warm places
Places that feed you so well both your stomach
and heart feel full
Words that come after a full stomach are the kind-
est
I read all the sticky notes
Smile the widest looking at little hearts and cute
smiley faces
They are genuine and raw
Sticky notes don't care about who'll read them
How many will read them
They aren't perfect
But all of them are pretty
They make you feel good
About a place
A place that feels like home
So the next time I see you...
Can I write you a sticky note?

DAKSHA

I spend most of my time reading books, watching every genre of movie, being excited about the fresh new leaf my favourite plant grew, daydreaming, imagining myself in the halls of Hogwarts or as the female lead of John Green's next novel.

When I'm not doing any of those, I am coding to pay my bills and as opposed to popular opinion I actually like my 9 to 5 job. (10 to 7, but play along)

Oh and I write sometimes!

I write when I have too much going on.
I write when I have too little going on.
I write to feel, to let out, to be understood by others, to understand myself better.
I believe words, like many other forms of art, are a way in which humans relate to one another, reach out to one another, even if they have never crossed paths.

Flip the page/scroll/swipe to read something I wrote one Saturday morning. It's about an emotion/a process we all struggle with.

MOVE ON

21 June 2013

"Hey, it's Daniel! I'm away. Leave a message".

Alana hears his quirky voice on the phone.

"It's Allie, umm calling to ask you to get off work early, I got something for you! So, get done early, will you?"

She had already looked up his calendar for the week and was planning to surprise him with a vacation to Mauritius. Just the two of them. She would be dropping off her 4-year-old Tracy at her in-laws. Her whole plan was in place.

Ever since Daniel had read the book "Following the equator" by Mark Twain, he had been wanting to visit Mauritius.

In Mr Twain's own words, 'Mauritius was made first, and then heaven; and heaven was copied after Mauritius.'

Alana had looked up the pictures of the place and boy! The author sure wasn't lying!

They boarded the flight that evening from New Orleans airport.

The flight attendant announced there would be slight turbulence in the air. Turbulences due to monsoon were pretty common around this time of the year, Daniel explained to a fear-struck Alana.

But as time passed, the slight turbulence turned out to be not so slight and soon the cabin-crew was preparing them for the worst-case scenario.

Before Alana could even realize what was happening she found herself plummeting through the air, falling down to Earth from 30,000 feet.

27 August 2013

She woke up with a jerk! Her pillow covered in sweat, her breathing heavy and her heart thumping.

"Okay okay. That was just a dream. Nothing happened.

Just a dream. Just a dream. Just a dream."

She turned over to tell Daniel about the nightmare, only to find his side of the bed empty.

'How do you wake up from a nightmare when you're not asleep?'

Every single moment came rushing back to her. How she had found herself in the jungle after the crash. How she kept calling out to him in the hope that she would hear him shout back "Allie!". How hours later she gave up hopes and started rummaging through wreckage. Maybe he was still there. Maybe he was just unconscious. Maybe he was too tired to shout for help.

She then lay on the bed staring at the ceiling, cursing herself.

It was her fault.

Daniel would still be alive if she had planned the trip for some other day. If she had chosen some other flight. If she had chosen some other place. If Daniel had not read the book "Following the equator".

If. If. If.

Her train of thought broke when Tracy jumped into bed and cupped her cheeks.

"Mommy! Were you crying?"

Alana quickly gathered herself up. Pulling Tracy into her arms she whispered, "No sweetheart. Mommy was just missing daddy. Do you miss him too?"

"Yes, mommy. A lot!"

Alana then made up her mind to stop wallowing, to go to therapy that her mom had been suggesting, to join the support groups for widows, to read the books on how to deal with PTSD, to get rid of survivor's guilt. She decided to do everything she could to get better for Tracy, if not for herself. That's what Daniel would have wanted.

02 November 2018

5 years later, Alana had settled into the new life of being a single mom. She had gotten a job in the local community college. The mother-daughter duo had moved into a cosy one-bedroom apartment. Her life had become all about teaching, Tracy's school, her ballet and drama classes. Weekends were spent snuggled in bed watching 70's classics.

One evening as she was dropping Tracy to her ballet class, her trainer explained to her Tracy would be needing a pair of ankle weights for the next class. She made a mental note to scan through the storeroom for ankle weights, the ones that she herself had used as a little girl.

On reaching home, she started searching through the storeroom. She stumbled upon a box, found an aftershave cream among other stuff. She opened the lid to find finger marks from the last use still left on the surface of the cream. Daniel's.

Her world came crashing down around her.

And in this one fleeting moment, 5 years later, all the therapies and support groups and books and everything she had done to move on seemed fruitless.

No matter how much we convince ourselves that

we have moved on, No matter how much we have actually moved on, there will come a day when something minor will happen. Something really tiny and insignificant. Like smelling a whiff of a perfume, or crossing a café you used to hang out at, or seeing someone in a crowd wearing the same shirt your partner used to wear or just the way the sky looks during a sunrise.

At that moment, regardless of how many new people you have met, how many breath-taking places you have visited, how many birthdays and anniversaries and promotions you have celebrated, regardless of any of that, it will hurt. It will hurt like a bitch. And there'd be nothing that you would be able to do except feeling that pain. Because 'That pain demands to be felt.'

At that moment consider yourself the luckiest of the lot because you, my darling, had something / someone worth grieving.

Alana then started frantically going through all the old boxes. His briefcase, his books, his broken spectacles, his guitar, his basketball, then she found his phone.
She curled up on the carpet with tears streaming down her cheeks. She turned the phone on. She started playing his voicemail greeting on loop.
"Hey it's Daniel, I'm away. Leave a message."
"Hey it's Daniel, I'm away. Leave a message."
"Hey it's Daniel, I'm away. Leave a message."

~DPS

RAJASHREE DAS PURKAYASTHA

I am an Indian artist and poet, trying to capture human emotions and express my musings with brushes and pen. I write about love, healing, rebellion, faith, hope, grit, and success. Both poetry and art take me away from the chaos of the world into the solitude of my happiness.

The writers who inspire me are Jane Austen, Emily Dickinson, Keats, Wordsworth, and Alfa Holden.

I have two books in progress, intending to bring them out sooner. Just counting on blessings from the universe and creating ripples of hope and positivity.

Faraway Love

There are thousand street lights,
competing with each other,
to catch my attention.
 but my moon,
in his calm composure,
is the heart's desire.

Woman of Steel

Do not see her as broken.
She is made of grit
and wears survival with flair.
Like steel tampered in the fire
and with every blow of life's hammer,
she evolved stronger,
and more whole.

Happiness With People's Name
in the practice of easy ways,
your life becomes a tale of countless
'leaving and let go.'

they were happy with people's name,
that wanted to stay;
but you didn't know.

Portrait Poem
Maybe intimidating to you,
the obstreperous child within me.
she is a defiant riddle,
half chaos, half surreal.
and away from the world
of rules and lies;
she finds happiness
in flowers and butterflies.

PIYUSH SHARMA

WRITER'S HEART

The search of our lives, for the lasting explan-
ations,

in the deep vastness of the blank paperwhites,

is to experience the awe of discoveries

in a journey through time, all in between these
lines

guides the inner survivors, the "carriers of light"

to achieve immortality, for eternity to come

a price must be paid in-breaths and loneliness,

to be left alone in thoughtful abstruseness

in search with hope, without which no new
worlds would be born

Or the black and white would dreadfully dawn,

such- the ink must never stop, it's forbidden and
ever undone,

thus a writer's heart is a dying one.

HOPE and I

HOPE utters:

it's the way up, the arrow, now wake up

jack sparrow, no mission no marrow,

uncharted, destinations and dreams, a creator or borrowed?

better a failure than a coward, at least you take up and swallow,

drowning remains no sorrow at least you did what you followed.

I :

I don't wanna do it when I make shit up,

All I do is stir it and no facing up,

never did I changed, like the sea and the oceans,

I dig deep with devotion, still no change of emotions,

draining inch by inch but never do I die,

curse of life more like recursive life, a penny for your thoughts,

The bothered mind makes no difference, penance for what,

fighting thyself & to sew what you bought?

HOPE utters:

fruits from the tree of excuses taste true- but explosive,

no benefits you got, gimmick thoughtless plot,

bitter truth tastes no good, but it builds you a bod,

patience for creation, testimony to the Gods,

holding onto your roots, you must never forget,

past was only created because- you moved ahead.

I :

Oh! The voice in my head, the brainchild of imagination,

you put end to the commotion, Oh! Deity of Karma

through your wisdom I fly, all steps become an evolution,

carrying the weight of my trust, I took sail in this ocean,

of dreams and destinations, a comrade for life,

an unknown explanation, I will try and try,

Until I.............................

मन?

मन?

शिकायत और कल्पना का दिलचस्प रिश्ता है,

जैसे संतुष्टि को मंजूरी के समान समझ लिया जाता है।

दिल की क्या ही करनी है सब मन ने हरा है।।

सभी मन की चाल है वही मस्तिष्क की ढाल है,

तलाश की छाओं में उम्मीदों को बटोरता,

अफसोस और तनाव का संजोगी जिस्म पर अज़ाब है।

सूरत से निरपराध और खुदी से ऐतराज़ी? बेमिसाल है!

अदृश्य संचालक झूठा मनरोगी, मानव इसी का गुलाम है,

कहने को यह हमसफर, वहीं करता गुमराह है,

जन्नत की लालसा देता, मात्र कपटी पनाह है।

साँसों में अल्फ़ाज़ बुन रहा, अश्कों का असबाब यह,

ज़र्ब की ज़मानत, बेकदर दिल-ए-गुस्ताख़ यह,

जीतेजी अपाहिज व पायाब बनादे,

बग़ावत में क्यों बरतता है?

जब तेरा मुझसे ही वजूद है!

तो खुदगर्जी क्यों चुनता है?

इंतज़ार

हर रोज़ मौत से लड़ते हैं परंतु

जब जब मन घबराता है,

खुद को खुद से पूछता पाया है

न जाने कब आओगी अनकही

क्योंकी

बहुत मुलाकातें अभी बाकी हैं,

न साथ छोड़ना सिखाया किसी ने

कैसे ज़िन्दगी सिर्फ यादें बनजाती हैं,

अवसर दोगी या अचानक ही पुकारोगी,

सालों की नींद अभी बाकी है

सपनों ने जो जगाया रखा है मुझे,हमारी कमी का कुछ एहसास होगा

या पन्नों मे इतिहास होगा,

हज़ारों सवाल बेसुलझे ही रह जाएंगे,

हम भी कब तक ही मुस्कुराएंगे।।

JUHI RANI BARAD

Juhi Rani Barad is a student at Regional Institute of Education, Bhubaneswar pursuing Integrated BSc BEd currently. Ink and paper are her perfect hiding spot but you may find her on Instagram and Your-Quote as girl_with_quill128. You could spot her roaming around all poetry clubs of Bhubaneswar or debating on multiple stages across the state with great wrath but never talking to people over there. Make a playlist of Arijit Singh songs for her and she's up for a meet. Being a foodie, she is a strong believer of the fact that food is symbolic of love when words are inadequate. Her email address is juhiastronaut@gmail.com because even though she floats in her imagination, she feels it's zero gravity over there:))

1)

The only ugliness you could

find by just seeing someone is

your own prejudice towards the dark

skinned, fat or short people

who don't fit in your rigid

definition of beauty.

The only beauty you could

find by just looking at someone

is the reflection of your own

inner kindness and beautiful heart.

2)

How low are we setting the bar
for intolerance towards dissent?
Dissent is not anti-national,
it's the most patriotic thing
in fact. Helping the nation to
improvise itself by pointing out
and discussing its flaws is always
better than living in a dream world,
chest-thumping about the glorious past.
Diversity of opinions is the beauty
of democracy, don't ruin it.

3)

"How are you?"

"I am fine."

"Tell me how are you really. What's not fine?"

"It feels like there is a

Titanic of my fake self-control

which had suddenly collided with the

Ice Berg of reality that hit really hard. Now I am amidst the Ocean of my own emotions,

sinking slowly with my illusionary Titanic"

4)

I have lost count of

People entering my life on the pretext of

Decorating the barren land of my heart,

Nullifying effects of previous treacheries,

Promising companionship till last breath.

But all ending up magnifying that scar of scary past.......

5)

Despite the days drenched in despondence,

There's something that keeps the flame awake.

Despite the nights, the pillows are wet,

There's something that bends the lip line wide.

Despite the ways, they try to make us cry,

There's something that dries those deary tears in our eyes.

Despite the times the heart wanted to be shattered,

There's something that joins back it tight.

Despite every cruel answer that compels me to move,

There's something that arises a curious question asking to stay back. Despite the nights spreading the darkest sorrows,

There's something that preaches our faith in the sunrise.

6)

Can you please open the lock of

my soul by unzipping my lips with

the key of your lips and explore

the deep world inside me that's

untouched and unexplored till date?

Your touch, scent and even voice

send signals to my brain to campaign

against working in all domains
blocking all other senses and make
their way through my veins to reign
over my heart. How can I ever pour
these into words as beads of poetry?

7)

Crave to carve out some scintillating perfection
in our bleak and black sky of doubts.

8)

Let the scribbling of pen on paper
be the voice of our soul
Let the smooth absorption of ink by paper
reflect the satisfaction of our heart
for being completely expressed

9)

I want to
Wiggle under your skin
Crawl into your mind and
Intoxicate your heart.

GUNJAN RATHOR

This is Gunjan Rathor on the other side of the page. Little girl with big dreams. An author of 'The First Steps' and a Doctor to be.

From Raipur, Chhattisgarh. Presently in 12th standard. Little girl with big dreams.
I was appointed as the member of STUDENT WRITERS CLUB of St. Joseph's Sr. Sec. School - a huge platform created by our Reverend Father Principal, Dr John Xavier. Also in the year 2018, I had the golden opportunity to be the Art And Design Editor of the magazine 'Tulika'.

The main reason why I started writing poems is that I want to express my high thoughts and deep feelings; it gives a feeling of liberation and a sense of elation. Writing is the best way to express our thoughts and feelings. When we write down our fantasies and dreams they become real and tangible.

~Gunjan Rathor

You Complete Me

The fragrance of yours refreshes me,
Each kick in your smile represents me,
No one can stop me being thee,
Happy lovelies in together we.

Your heart keeps on soothing me,
Your talks keep on nourishing me,
No comfort could match your embrace,
Your company raise me to serve an ace.

You are my dose of satisfaction,
You complete me with all affection.
Your efforts light up the bond.
There's no other love of which I'm fond.

~Gunjan Rathor

To Be Blessed

An occult I found,
Mom-Dad wishes a baby who is all around.
Not the abnormal case,
I was born something to chase.
You put a smile on the face,
I born to give flick on the human race.
Normal you are, later inflict by guardians.
I was curse inside the womb of my companion.
At the drop of a hat, I speak,
Great innovation was given by this beak.

Not a hot potato, God doesn't cheat,
The flying one doesn't require feet.

~Gunjan Rathor

Optimistic She

The alarm screamed,
wailing to wake me up.
It was dawn,
rising to shake me up.
With the final pages, I stood,
digesting as much as I could.
The stars glowed.
I walked on the street.
My steps paused.
My feet forgot their beat.
Interference of white snowy face,
Roasted me to serve an ace.
You girl staring me, behind Tannen,
In the dark about traffic Canon.
Being the culprit, he shouted on innocent,
Being guiltless I didn't accept his ascent.

I roar, I argued, I abused by defaults,
A girl with a voice, A lady without faults!

~Gunjan Rathor

Way I See It

Life has a versatile inflexion,

It's you who can handle the situation.
Grumpy one is not ill-temper.
These people only need to be pampered.
Yes, women out there are groggy,
They never responded to enraged froggy.
Seven stages don't ask you to grovel,
But definitely to shine like marble.

~Gunjan Rathor

SABIYA PATHAN

"Among other things, you'll find that you're not the first who was ever confused and frightened and even sickened by human behaviour "J.D Salinger

I'm Sabiya Pathan, working as an HR in IT Company in Pune, Completed MBA from MIT.

Basically, I put love into words and help you connect with the people and moments that matter. It's always said that receive without pride and let go without attachment. It's always not too late to start something. Months passed by and by and several things have changed in my life, that is my relationship and I'm still hoping to get things better soon, my dreams, attachment towards family, goals and most important my career.

I'm such a person that always keep my thing with me and I don't complain, and I don't expect much from the people around me.

And this is the thing that has bothered me in my entire life, soon started to write and peen down my emotions and feelings into words. My journey of becoming a writer is full of frustrations, good experiences but also full of hope. Everyone who deserves it should get a chance to narrate themselves.

I learned from a lot of people and still in touch with both kinds of people.

Before I end this, I also want to tell everyone who is reading this "Never lose hope, there is sun after rain and love after pain"

Sabiya Taslim Pathan

Writer, Pune

Spread Positivity

It's been more than 150 days we are stuck in one place and the world just stopped.
This year no matter what was very difficult for everyone.
Some lost their loved ones and just shattered into pieces.
This year was a roller coaster ride for everyone.
A virtual hug to everyone who's trying their best just to at peace
It's just a phase and this will shall pass too.
I understand you!
Spread positivity and love!!

Ex BestFriend

Days have passed by and so as you. Sometimes I still scroll through pictures of us and smile.
I don't think there will ever be a day when I don't cross my mind at least once.
Just know that I don't hate you and that i'll always loves you!
#ExBestFriend

Change

Every day is a chance to change yourself to be a better human Being.

Berang

Rang badalti hui duniya main
Mujhe apna berang hona pasand aaya!

Just a reminder

Someday you will have so much of light inside you
that you will run out of places to put it!
one more good thing and you will be overflowing.

Better Tomorrow

It's okay if today you feel all alone or disturbed
It's okay if today didn't have a productive day
It's okay today you just relax in the bed with some
coffee watching your favourite movie
All days are not the same
Some days are just to hug yourself and treat our-
selves better for a better tomorrow!

Miracles do happen

The most beautiful part is
I wasn't even looking when I found you.

We fight every day

We fight a battle every single day no one is aware
of.
It's not always you will win, sometimes you have
to face failure
In life, you will come across many obstacles but
remember you are born strong and you can fight
every battle of your life.
Life is a roller coaster ride, It's fun but someone's
it's painful too.
We are born in such a generation where we find
peace and enjoyment in making fun of others,
gossiping, back bitching, sharing your rubbish
thoughts on someone's friendship and relationship status.
Always remember to make people feel good about
themselves.
Don't stop dreaming just because you had a nightmare.

Just understand the meaning between social anxiety and attitude.
Be a good listener, try to connect with your loved

once and try to dig out the things which are eating them up so badly.

Try to make them calm and no matter what the situation is try to listen to them.

Be kind to even smiling faces.

Sometimes things may get worst and worst and you will not find a way but have faith and hope everything is going be okay soon.

Don't be Judgemental! People will never tell you the whole story, Sharing your rubbish opinions on someone is very easy and fun nowadays.

But you will never feel what the person is going through.

If that person has reached out to you so somewhere you definitely hold a special place in their life, So be a good listener and dig out the topic that is eating them up.

Passing comments is very easy but if you go through the same situation then you understand the real pain.

Always remember everyone has an untold story to share with you and with everyone.

When the ego relaxes we can meet others with clarity, awareness and presence.

Learn to love some people from a distance and find peace within.

Keep everyone in your prayers as you remember them in your gossips.

Don't allow toxic thoughts to hold you to ransom.

Be a free bird and enjoy every bit of what you are doing and find peace while doing that.

Be kind to everyone!
Remember there is sun after rain and love after
pain.
So
I'm holding on because God is my hope.

VIDUSHI SHRIVASTAV

My name is Vidushi Shrivastava and
I am 18 years old. It has been 3 years that I've been writing and with every new day, I learn some more about me, the world and love.

I have always felt that there are two things that make a writer

1.   A lot of reading
2.   A broken heart

With everything that you read that I have written, you'll know that I belong to the second part more than the first one. Love and pain have taught me a lot and most importantly made me grow out of it. I have learnt innumerable things metaphorical and realistic with every passing day. Yes, I am just 18 and what do I know about love? Or the world and its people?

Love, I feel is persistent. The person might leave, the story might not complete. But love, it always stays. It reminds you of that one person, with every breath you take, and it never leaves. It lessens but never leaves.

These writings are for that person.
And you, to live a story.
Love,
Heer.

The empty roads have more stories to tell than anyone
They have heard,
They have heard it all
A girl talking to herself,
Parents talking about work and problems
Someone wondering about the next day
A guy, planning his conversation
A couple walking but quiet, thinking about the downs
Those roads know them in real
And the sky knows,
What they wish for looking at it
How dearly they pray,
In spite of having some good amount of friends and people to talk,
We share to those, who keep it within.
The empty roads and the limitless skies
Hold the real us,
And here we are,
Glad they cant speak to the world.

____

When a broken soul writes,
The world,
Experiences a shiver down their spine
And the sky tends to break its beauty
the grass isn't green and
It burns down to ashes
When a broken soul writes,

You feel what they did.
You tremble
Because when she writes
You know something broke her
And you're afraid
To see what happens.

——————

Why do you feel so far today?
Those little things mean too much, don't they?
 I told you, I was nothing but your love,
Always knowing my beyond
My flesh knows your smell too true,
My heart does not grieve the sorrow any more, it
drank it like wine and turned it to blood gushing
in my veins.
My feet so cold, still afraid to touch yours
So, I turn to my side of the bed, knowing that I
should sleep too
The corners feel too close,
You still feel far.
Just like the moon on that night
Quiet, admirable and unknown.

——————

All the seasons
We 've spent together
This one, without you
is longer than any

The sun brings your warmth on a cold winter morning
and the birds make me think of your voice
When leaves shed, this autumn
I thought about how I was never afraid to fall for you,
how we were never afraid to get crushed like the leaves
knowing they'll bloom again
But this one,
It feels longer than usual
Heavier and
Ironically, empty.

TANYA ZANZAD

Myself Tanya Zanzad, a 17-year-old teenage girl preparing and planning to create and crack as many opportunities I can because I just want to be happy in life. I'm really fascinated by failure and success stories. I'm kind of introvert who doesn't like to interact with people. If I had a choice between attending parties and read books sitting back at home it's for obvious I'm gonna choose reading books. I was just 10 when I got to know about my hearing defect, but then I was just a kid who knows nothing about this problem. But when I enter my teenage years it has affected my daily life badly. My relatives and mom's friends were like they showed me sympathy for my loss, They will always say that I'm sorry for your child she can't do anything. At the point they were correct but even then I realized when one has the will, power, and determination then you can do anything that you dreamt to be. As I grow up my life became a challenge because when you are one of those people who can't hear properly you are definitely gonna have a great time dealing with talking to people around.   At the age of 14, I read about Helen who was similar to me. I always admired Helen Keller and fully expected her to accomplish a great thing. Sometimes we run behind the memories we loved a lot but, We have to accept that these are just memories because all time remembering these will give us only pain. I know it's not easy to move on or forget them because totally, they are impossible but we have to do it for persons who really care for us they all just want to see us happy and we hide all these things from them so be happy and find happiness from all around us they are hidden all around us just we have to see them.

I love to read write my own thoughts and spread love but sometimes I end up spreading sadness in form of my writings. I'm sorry about that.

I started self-doubting myself, and then I realize I was wrong all thanks to my friend to put some brains in me. So I ended up writing this letter for myself.

Dear 17-year-old Me,

I hugged you and praised you and appreciated you for the wondrous person you are–for all the beauty and life you bring to this world.

I seldom tell you how much I love you. How much I admire you. How beautiful and caring and intelligent and strong you are. That you are my hero. (point no.1 love yourself). I loved the way you do not care what others think, not be afraid to be different, not be ashamed of who you are.

Worst of all, I said you're not enough. That if you'd only be, a better daughter, a better friend, a better writer, a better lover...then I'd love you. If you were more confident, more social, more assertive, then I'd respect you. If you had fewer sunspots, if you ate fewer carbs, if you achieved your goals, then I'd want you. I've said things to you I wouldn't say to my worst enemy and you've taken it, and internalized every calloused word.

And for that, I've lost you. I lost myself. I'm so incredibly sorry I failed you. I'm sorry for hurting you, for leaving you, for not reminding you every second of every day how wonderful you are. How worthy you are? How brave and kind and powerful you are? Please forgive me.

YOU are significant.
YOU are worthy.
YOU are beautiful.
YOU are smart.
YOU are strong.
YOU are enough.

You do not need anyone else's approval, love or friendship to be whole.
Together WE are enough. We will conquer this new future. I've got you and this time I'm not letting go. Ever. This time, I will put you first.

I know you are going through hard times right now. That life hasn't given you what you hoped and hasn't turned out the way you thought it would. I know you are disappointed and sometimes feel like a failure or that it is all your fault. But the truth is: YOU are not a failure nor could you ever be. YOU are strong and brave and honest and YOU will overcome. YOU will persevere and come out on the other side more YOU than you've ever been before. hugged you and praised you and appreciated you for the wondrous person you are–for all the beauty.

I will respect you and honour you and cherish you.
Love for eternity,
Me

My friends find me as their motivational agent (laughs) believe me I'm absolutely not I just put forward my theories of life. I and my friends were in 10th and so we were stressed about board exams, and at the point of time my best friend was freaking out unnecessarily. There I came to know I need something to do about her unnecessary freaks because I know her problems have perfect solutions and she can figure out herself but at the end, she will depend on me to give her much needed boost. So I wrote this letter to her secretly and the next day she came to me smiling tension free. My best friend is a total extrovert and I'm total introvert so as we have different personalities this letter is just a token of love for her.

Dear best friend:

For best friends, we couldn't be more different in personality. Your outgoing, loud, and social persona rivals my reserved and hesitant disposition. But, I'm as thankful for you as I am different from you. Nobody could ever replace you in my heart and in my life.
I know you know this. I'm quick to tell you of my appreciation and, but I want to take a minute to highlight all the exceptional things you do for me. Thank you for all the quiet evenings in. I can't tell you enough how blessed I am to have a friend who's perfectly okay having a movie marathon or just sitting together.

Thank you for being tolerant of how often I zone out. And thank you for patiently repeating the stories of school when I couldn't actually hear properly. Thank you for always leaving social gatherings early, even when I politely insist on staying. I'm willing to stay because I think it's beautiful how you light up when you're around people, but I also appreciate how you know when my tolerance for people has reached the max. . If there's one thing I can't stand as an introvert, it's when someone is overbearing. Thank you for comforting me in just the right amount and always being there when I need you. Thank you for consistently using your vibrant personality to make me laugh and smile. You've got enough personality for the both of us, and it keeps me glowing and going.

Thank you for forcing me to get out there every once and awhile. Because of you, I'm able to hold my own at a social event (even if that means awkwardly sitting there until approached). Without you, I would spend all my days inside the home. Thank you for being okay with me telling you that I'm just not feeling like hanging out. Most people get offended when I say this. You, on the other hand, tell me it's okay and let me know when you're available next to me

And most of all, thank you for being one of the only people I can stand to be around. For never ruining my energy levels. And for always keeping me company. I know this isn't something you can help. You just happen to be my person by chance. But I am still forever grateful to have found the person that keeps me going.

Nervous and frustrated about your boards well that's the universal reaction of every board appearing students mine too.........

But remember........

The Ladder in success is never easy, But you must strive to climb up. It just requires undivided attention towards your goals. Give in all the power that you have. There will be situations that may bring you down, your hard work can overcome any obstacle. YOU just have to BELIEVE. Have listened that DREAM IS NOT WHAT YOU SEE IN SLEEP BUT SOMETHING WHICH DOESN'T LET

YOU SLEEP
There will be times when you will feel lost and
low,
But let's remember one thing guys we started this
for a purpose only to achieve our dreams. It's okay
to rest for a while but never give up.

There's always away. If you can dream it, do it,
then achieve it
Stop complaining and have self-confidence
It's all about the state of mind if others can do it
then we too.

Soon you will enter the age where society will
start judging you
But remember that society is no one to judge your
life don't let them affect so much to you.
Just face every situation with a kickass smile.

So my dear friend let's get up,
Pull up your shirt sleeve.
And be ready to face the situations
And let's write our own destiny.

Love
Tanya

AISWARYA SHILPA J

I am Aiswarya Shilpa J, born and brought up in Kerala. I did my schooling in Holy Trinity School, Palakkad, Kerala. As a school student, I was very interested in writing poems, essay and also loved to participate in recitation competitions in the school, district and state levels and also had the blessing to gain positions and certificates. Being raised by loving and supportive parents, grandparents and a whole of a wonderful family; I was always motivated and appreciated for every little thing I did and that made me stronger day by day, it made me have the strong wanting to do more and more of things even which was beyond my capacity. As a student, I was always geared up by my teachers and every single friend of mine too contributed to making me a strong and confident person.

Later, I took up commerce and that gave me a clear picture into the entrepreneurial concepts and the various ideas of business, I was eager to know about success and failure stories of different entrepreneurs and that made me write and have my own interpretations on failure and the related success. After I finished my schooling I joined Amrita University, Ettimadai, Tamil Nadu, wherein I joined for my BA English degree course. One question that would come to any person's mind is why I chose English, my mother being an English teacher and my family supporting me to learn more and to always have a fascination for the language, I was trained well enough to speak and write English, this made me have an interest towards the same.

From times when I used to write poems and quotes in the back pages of my notebook, I took up the chance of logging in to the app named Your quote, which made me have a greater and increased passion towards writing, I found that there were a lot of prompts provided on daily basis, I started writing even more and later also started an Instagram account for my writings. Presently, I am doing my final year degree and in the meanwhile, I never wanted to drop my passion for writing and still continues to write and would always do the same.

The glow of sunset

And before the tired sun hid behind

The mountains, as I could see.

It brought in a glow, brightness,

A glow that even the fresh sun

Of a pleasant morning could not provide.

And this light lighted up the whole room

And later gave way to –

The bright moon of the dark sky.

The beauty of an evening

The setting sun looked proud.

The silver lining was highlighting the cloud.

The trees kept swaying as if they were –

Impressed by the power of the wind.

And ignoring all the responsibilities –

I was shouldered with,

I went up to the rooftop and gave in myself,

To this unexplainable beauty of nature.

MISTY MORNING

This morning I woke up to not find the sun.

Instead, there was mist and it knew, it made the sight unclear.

But for my mind adored the same,

Despite the fact that I could not have a proper image –
Of what was present behind the misty outside,
It took away my worries and hid them behind,
Just like a baby hiding her toy and blushing
When the rest of the world keeps searching.

WAKE UP

The breeze escaping from under the door
The sun shines with delicacy
And the light hitting the corners
It is beauty for sure
But to enjoy it-
One should wake up,
Wake up from under the crumpled blanket.

AT NIGHT, MY MIND FLOATS

After the whole day of work
After the not so heavy dinner
I slowly settle down.
I read it was nice to sum up-
All nice things that,
The day has given you
And thank Almighty for everything.
I do all of it & find the happiness of my own.

I slowly go to bed, set my alarm
Glad at the eight hours remaining for the ring
I decide to close my eyes and sleep.
But here comes the thoughts,
All piled up ones
I find my mind getting hyperactive
I get all weird thoughts then,
I soon get up & start walking,
Checking if the moon is still in the sky,
Start peeping through the window
To count the stars
And end up –
Counting the number of homes where-
Lights are turned off
And people are sleeping happily.
At night my mind floats
Just like a paper boat on the water.

BHAVITHA THIPPANNA

I am a 24-year-old aspiring Data Scientist. Born and raised in Bangalore my interests and zest for the English language started after my school, as a teenager I've always been fond of reading. Like any other teenager who is hopelessly romantic, Chetan Bhagat was something that I read first. My genre would be romance and I do like Durjoy Dutta's work. I enjoy the mystery as well Murakami is my favourite. I volunteered and worked for Non-Profit Organizations sharing my knowledge with them and discussing sensitive and life-oriented topics. Of late I moved to Melbourne for my further studies, spending time for myself and with experiences I had there, I let myself to explore the talents that I always thought I had. Initially, I was experimenting with my captions on Instagram.

Poetry is a completely new venture for me and when I recited my sample ones to my friends they insisted that I should put it out for the public. Now I enjoy writing it and reciting them, although currently, I do it as a hobby, one day I wish to take it to another level and maybe be an avid poetess. I do like writing short stories as well.

Find some of my best works here.

To follow me on social media:

Instagram & Facebook : @terribly.poetic

Blog : https://terribly-poetic.blogspot.com/

God's own creation

It's amazing to see how strong you pretend, it's that heart that you always have to tend.
Every morning you look for a new scope, but why do you even try something that you cannot cope.
Don't strain that little heart of yours to keep up, slowdown sometimes it's good to take time to catch up.
Regardless of how hard you try, there's always someone out there who love's to see you cry.
Where's the race? Whom are you trying to impress?
There! Stop right there and say this to yourself "I'm the best and I don't care about the rest".

'Cause my love, you're god's own creation, and you don't need any incarnation.
Dance a little, smile a little, and cry a little..... Oh, that joy is a bundle.
You know that you are vulnerable, stop pretending to be a rebel.
'Cause my love, you're god's own creation, and you don't need any incarnation.

Music is MAGIC!

Ah, music you're magic!
Sometimes the world around us looks like a big hole,
And then you come and heal any damaged soul.
After one long day that makes me wanna cry,
A perfect music kicks in going..... Do you wanna let me try?
Beiber to Swift, Mendes to Puth, Ed Sheeran.... you're just what I wanna hear.
'Cause these days are going like, something I cannot bear.
Lonely rides I've got covered, party all night I've you covered.
Ok, fine! It's extremely poetic! Well, that's what music is.

Have you tried staring at the stars while music soothes your ears all night, especially on those days where your schedules are uptight?
Music is a gift to be embraced and memories that you don't want to have erased.
Take your pick and indulge in your kind of music, 'cause you know... Music is magic!

....oh but without letting you know!

When my friend first told me about you I didn't care, unless I heard those compliments that touched I thought that was fair.

Well, while that went on I looked upon you, intriguing I thought and told my friend that I would want to know you.

Oh man, I went head over heels when we hit it off in the first go, I was so glad when we had those chats in a row.

But my heart broke when you told me that there's another girl in that heart of yours, 'cause I thought now that I had no chance.

Well, that didn't dull my feelings for you, hence I gave my heart in spending time with you.

My heart kept sinking in while you constantly mentioned her, lest I always gave you the advice to impress her.

'Cause baby, I was falling for you now.... oh but without letting you know.
You flirted with me I let happen, yet you spoke of her I let happen.
'Cause baby, I was falling for you now..... Oh but without letting you know.
That bliss of your text, that comment you left, this heart that felt, ah how can you spend all that time with me and yet not feel for me.

Of course, your heart was full of her, hence I told you that I had a crush on you to see if that heart would let me in instead of her.

Wow, you played it well again by liking me as a friend, but darling I dreamt to be your girlfriend.

Nevertheless, I was glad we at least spoke as friends, but days went by and we ended up not even being friends.

Now here we are wishing each other on birthdays, but mind you I think of you on all days.

'Cause baby, I love you now..... Oh but without letting you know.

My friend, you are so dear.

How often do you get to meet someone relatable, stuck with you despite all the trouble?

Days and nights, sometimes all day long, you wanna spend all the time with them along.

You fight with them, you fight for them, oh but you cannot live without them.
Some are crappy some are dumb, for all you care each one is a treasured gem.

Moments with them are always cherished, losing anyone of them is a pain that cannot be perished.

Oh, friend, you are so dear. Without you in it, my life is fear.

I cry I shall survive, 'cause you're here to alert me

of those troubles and revive.

You say you hate me, but no buddy I ain't gonna give up on you.
'Cause my mate you never did when I was you.

You know me better than I do myself, clearly, we are better shrinks to each other than to ourselves.

Leeches we are to each other, oh yes! We make the best team together.

And that's because my friend you are so dear, gosh but sometimes you are such a fear!

VRUSHAL VAGHELA

"Some stories don't need a complete ending, that's my poem".

A young boy from Gujarat studying Computer Engineering at ITM Universe.

Studying is not a major part of me, but writing poems, doing social work at two NGOs named Lights of Hope and The Feeders Club which basically educates unprivileged poor children and feeding stray dogs respectively. Very curious about doing some new stuff and exploring unknown things.

Not much interested in engineering but found passion in my words.

I believed that when you have a broken heart you will find something outside of

Your mind to divert your heart. But when you observe and find something in your mind You will find your real purpose. That purpose will become your passion.

That's what happened to me. My broken heart

made me write poems and now I want to lead my words to another level. Hoping to see new opportunities.

Night Little Longer

We held the night a little longer,
Grasping breath together,
But divided by screens, oh! Modern love,
In oceans of love & deserts of thoughts,
There was that new traveller crossed,
Huge hand of the clock was passing, slowly,
Coming moment to profess love, closely,

Aah wait,
heavy breath with smell of afraid,
What's that?
Fear to shatter the dreams we made?
She dares to let flow the magical words to my shore,
Tears shed first then my words, before,

I like a lonely moon, & she my brightest star,
Brighten up my life like the whole sky.

Dried Love

Going Back in the Calendar,
I saw a rose with a lavender.

Where I carried my guts and reached in an instant,
I saw her in red from a distant,
Delivered romantic leaflet over a cappuccino,
While her juicy cheeks turned into a tomato,
Accompanied her lips,
With her smile of colour baby pink.

Not uttered a word, but her action spoke loud
enough,
And her smile had a gesture of accepting my stuff.

But now my shout is unheard,
And her feeling got zip covered,
Today the rose is dried,
and the letter is ripped,
But my words never lied,
and still, my heart is clipped.

Though our love is my honour,
However, I weep my tears in a corner

Golden Sky Over my Mind

She living, at the golden sky there,
Where bloom, the blossom of care,
Thou pretty round face possess glow,
That the instance I gaze her everything goes slow,
Her glowing skin is so fair,
That I can't half my eyes to stare,
Voice of her
Is like romantic music on the radio,
Which I'll never resist listening to her audio,
Mushy hand outstretch her lips
as she smiles, shy,
That drives my tummy
Full of the butterfly,
Just the imagination of her,
Takes my dream to her. That how come?
I can hear her heart beating in my poem.

Chaos in My Mind

While driving by the memory lane,
We heard a song together,
Now that tune is making my mind insane,
Still, I bury my head and missing the weather.
My shuffled playlist is hitting my ears,
But I am sobbing by that melody,
Yet my eyes are having dried tears,
And that music is becoming my enemy.
Presently, My heart is blind,
All I have is chaos in my mind.

AAYUSH ACHARYA

Hi, I'm Aayush, I am a final year Automobile engineering student, currently studying in ITM(sls) Baroda University, Vadodara. I am really passionate about writing, My content is mostly dark, fantasy and intense. I love to write experiences of life which we face in our lives but are difficult to express, how we make a small moment into a big moment of happiness, and how our mind reacts at a difficult situation and the way we overcome every problem in our life. I dedicate these writings to you, the readers. May you learn from this small experience I have faced and discover your true self.

Cave of emotions

I walked,
Into the arms of darkness.
A cave,
Which was nothing but a house of evil.
I struggled,
To find that light of hope.
I failed,
Lost into the darkness I felt pain.
I remembered,
All the good times I enjoyed with myself.
I felt that guilt,
The people I have hurt unwilling.
I realized,
Responsible for my actions was no one but me.
I gave up,
I found nothing but I willing to give up.
I saw,
The light of hope, a door of trust.
I believed,
The good side of mine has paid off.
I entered,
Through the door to the new chapter of life.

– Aayush Acharya

The lost path

The journey was smooth, but different was the
emotion.

I tried to be strong, but the emotions were cruel.

I learned to be brave, but difficult was the path.

I felt love which was broke into parts.

life was difficult but strong was my soul

at every path there was a ghost to hunt,

my brain took a step back, but my heart was strong.

I broke apart but the destiny kept me calling,

louder and stronger was her voice,

life took all of me except my soul.

the moment I realized nothing mattered but my path of success.

– Aayush Achary

Phase

Love.

That weird feeling which we experience, that feeling which lies within us, that feeling which can't be described in words. The love which we believe will last long, the promise made to love till eternity, all the promises made to be fulfilled. The dreams we saw together to be with each other, that birthdays celebrated together, to celebrate the unconditional love, that late-night calls telling each other how much we meant to each other, falling more and more in love. That dates, we went walking throughout the night covered with stars, holding each other's hand and thanking God for blessing them with the perfect partner which are now the perfect soulmates.

All broken down.

The promises, the memories, the bond, the love all broken down. It's really hard to tell whose fault was it. It was her fault or mine, hard to identify, still crying till dawn, and regretting if I had just talk with her one last time things would be different now, she still would be with me, but realizing at the moment that all the things are long gone now. You could do nothing but regret. But yes, I still recall the good memories which stay with me forever.

And that's love.

-Aayush Acharya

Dreams

Dreams, an unknown virtual reality

The dreams which we experience while escaping from the reality, living in our own imaginary world of happiness and sorrow, things we wish, we could have in our real life, things we want to eliminate from our life, things we want to achieve in our life, the things which are hard to achieve but still we want to pull those things out.

We dream about the mistakes we have made, the people we have hurt knowing or unknown, we wish if we had a chance to correct those things, life would be different.

We fight, we cry, we lose, we win, we experience everything and not once in the moment we have no idea this is just a dream, everything is gonna be over tomorrow.

Waking up in the morning, having that confused thoughts in our mind, thinking wow, what a beautiful lie it was, but still remembering everything in the dream playing the dream again and again in our mind, having an unknown satisfaction, smiling and saying, ' at least, I am happy in my dream'.

-Aayush Acharya

SNEHA S NAIR

I am Sneha S Nair, hailing from Palakkad, Kerala. I have completed my graduation from college of engineering chengannur. I am currently working in a reputed private firm. I really want to engage in social issues especially women, transgender issues. Through my poems, I am trying to empower the people who have lost the courage to go miles to attain the cherry of triumph.

Scented oilcans

Going downstairs
With those
furrows in my brow
Fascinated the concept
Of seeing the grave.
Oilcans were arranged
Row wise,
Parasites unleashed
It's emancipation through
The holes in the walls
Gravels pervaded
Resembling goat droppings.
Bones of dead ones slept,
Snoring at the uncertain
Look of mine.
Unrequited love,
Shown by those papers
Glued over the outer portion
Of oilcans.
Never found out the grave
That I was searching for
Those scented oil cans
Gave a glittery glimpse
Death bells rang
You know, my dark soul
Life starts from these
Scented oil cans,
Continues to the uncanny
Paths filled with flowers,

Throne of the mausoleum,
Then to the utter freedom
The freedom that breeze
Experience to kill
Someone with toxic smoke
And lick someone's body
With an amorous tongue
Those wells, with scented
Oils,
Gave me the charm of a lover
You my dark soul, you
Made me the last letter of this
Intricate nature.

Scarlet wings

To those brave girls,
who dazzled like a cinder
To those vivified heads
and untamed hearts
To those hairs braided
with a ribbon of boldness
To those sagacious ones
who realize they have a
vertebral column not
to stoop but to stand proudly
To those cathartic cries they
had in their pillow
To wipe out it with

That much intensity...
You have an antidote
within you
Truly speaking
Those scarlet tinged
wings are not for the
ground seekers
but for the ones
who really desires to roam
You are that masterpiece
destined to roam around
the amber of your passions.
That's you,

Breaking beauty

You can't define beauty
By those curved eyebrows
And strawberry-scented lip
Balms, the curve of the hips
And tangled front hairs
You can't say her hot
Only by looking into the
Transparent skin that is soon
Going to be ashes
You can't define her mood
As a pleasant one
When she struggles with
Rape misinterpreting as
Orgasms only because
You tied her a knot

Or you gonna do that
You can't call her
Uncompromising only
Because she resisted
The series of lusts you
Want to glorify through
The partner's cobwebs
Haven't u seen spiders?
She never will be a spider
And you never want her
To be a spider.
Why, because,
The world is full of thorny bushes
And she is misinterpreting
Marital rape as orgasms!
She is breaking her beauty
With a bleeding vagina
And don't hesitate
To call her complicated
Obviously, the cries are not
At all those goosebumps
It's the injury to her self pride

Besotted legs and trampled shadows

Daddy comes every day when the twilight
Bifurcates the light into shadows
Like a miscreant, grasshopper
Intrudes into the cracks of walls
Mom became a vociferous loudspeaker
Alcohol staggers inside his belly
Like the movement of a snake.
He never came that day
Mamma's hand froze with
Wheat flour and dough
My rapacious belly was ready to suffer
Starvation. And I thought
Where did Those besotted legs and trampled
Do shadows go?
It can't go to some other pastures
Some other homes,
It can't slap some other shoulders.
Myopic eyes often started to sew the dress
again enhancing the sartorial elegance.
I missed those shadows hued with that
Of pickles and spirit.
Still, I proclaimed:
Shadows have gone.
Light is yet to come.
Life is yet to start

Cherished desires

Maybe the day was forgotten

The warmth of the soil
has Been effaced.
Reflections of nightmare
Intoxicated the serene mornings
Existence of loving maniacs
Became unnecessary
Still, I see that smile
Holding that bunch of Memorabilia.
I could see the stars
Flowing through the river
Like our last conversation

NUPUR AWASTHI

She is a writer and a budding poet who spends her time buried in books and prefers the company of animals to humans! You will mostly find her daydreaming, and coffee mostly fuels her.

Dear first love

Yes, you broke my heart and it's been a long time since then.

At first, I was inconsolable. You were all I needed.

But then I healed, at which point? I cannot really tell.

Then, things that once looked bleak started looking well.

I started loving myself again and grew mentally fitter.

Because honestly, you broke me.

Without you, I was better.

I thought I was unfixable until I started working on me.

I was perfect and that I started to see

I still thought of you here and there,

But not so much as before because I really didn't care.

Now, you are just faded memories warning me of what not to do.

I still have issues trusting someone, but I somehow learn to do.

Looking in the mirror, I sometimes still hear your comparisons

Where you called her prettier and mocked my dusky skin.

No don't worry, I won't let your unsolicited comments win.

It's only now that I have come to love myself.

So I won't let the buried past hurt me more.

I know now, it's me I must love first.

I understand now, it's me I must put first.

So, thank you for teaching me things I didn't know before.

For helping me love myself a lot more than before.

- Nupur Awasthi

Redefining Perfection

Don't go out in sun, it will make you tan and dark,

I heard this from a young age,

Never realizing its harsh impact.

And then I grew, so did my weight,

Boys like slim girls and not curvy,

They told me again.

My wavy short hair was mocked again,

Men prefer long hair,

They told me this again.

But I am happy with the way I am,

Dusky, curvy perfection.

Love will find me as I am.

I won't change for him or her.

- Nupur Awasthi

Your Scars Are Beautiful

Show me all your scars,

Don't hide any of those marks.

I promise I won't judge,

I will accept each one, I won't budge.

It's time for us to love them all,

Don't hide yourself,

It's time to stand tall.

Those flaws are so very beautiful,

Each one tells a story that's meaningful.

We are all broken, life's a fight,

Don't be ashamed, it's alright.

I know, your heart is bruised,

I know, your soul is abused.

But together, we will rise.

We will battle it out, we will shine.

- Nupur Awasthi

I Am My Mother

I used to think I am better than her,

After all, I was the generation next.

But as I grew I found myself,

Mirroring her now and then.

I looked like her, I had her eyes,

That's what my father said.

My angry flare, also matched hers,

That's what grandma said.

I looked like her, loved like her,

I dressed in her sarees,

I moved like her.

I carried my mama's shadow within.

As I grew more I turned into her.

And that made me happier from within.

- Nupur Awasthi

Yash Jadhav

My name is Yash Jadhav and I am from Bombay. I'm a stock market aspirant, storyteller, writer, poet, author etc. My life is basically balanced between numbers and words i.e. stock market numbers and my poetic words. I'm a guy who grew up watching movies, which kinda made me fall for stories and also people's experiences have helped me to express my writings. I have been a part of an anthology before and would love to write and share millions of stories to the world for eternity.

साज़िशें ज़ुल्फ़ों की

जब उनके घुंगराले ज़ुल्फ़ों की लटे
हवाओं के साथ बहकर

उनके ही कामुक चहेरे पर ठेहर जाती थी,
तब लगता था मानों वक्त से लड़ कर
तथा हाथ घड़ी के कांटों को रुका कर
उन लटो को खुद से ही सजा दूं।
लेकिन उससे पहले ही
कम्बक्त उनकी उंगलियां,
तेज़ी से अपना काम कर जाती थी।
पर जनाब कुछ भी कहो
उन उंगलियों की भी क्या क़िस्मत,
जिन्हें उनकी ज़ुल्फ़ों में
उलज जाने का हक़ मिला।

MY POETIC PARADISE

In my poetic paradise,

you and I will be lying on our terrace.

Where you will be catching thunder

for our bedroom stories,

and I will try to steal the moon,

because I don't want to admire

anything more beautiful than you.

And after that, with your help

I can complete all of

my half-written poetries,

as every inch of your skin

is my favourite phrase.

So with your permission

can I kidnap you from

this real but plastic world

to my unknown poetic paradise?

कहानियां और वो

लोगों के शोरगुल के बीच,

इस खामोश शहर में।

कोई तो है शायद साथ मेरे,

परछाई सा जुड़ा हुआ,

गलियों और नुक्कड़ों से गुजरता हुआ।

कहे ना पाऊंगा यार उसे,

पर सुन तो लेगा वो

मेरे पैरों की आवाज अगर

कहीं रुक जाऊं गलती से ।

मैंने ठान तो लिया था कि

उसे अपने अनसुने कहानियों में

एक सुंदर अध्याय सा लिख दूं।

पर शायद किसने पहले हीं

वक्त को ठहराकर,

पक्के स्याही से,

मुझे हीं उसके सरल कहानियों

में एक उलझे हुए

किरदार सा लिख दिया हैं।

ONE MORE DANCE

In the middle of the night,
I found myself sitting
at my living room,
remembering the dance
we used to do

on your favourite
retro songs,

and I always liked the way
the world used to get quiet.

But now as
you are not here,

those songs doesnt haunt me,
in fact, they remind me of you,
your warm little fingers,
asking me for one more dance,
every time.

RICHA DEWANI

Young ambitious 20-year-old mind. Creative and innovative ideas to express in the most welcoming manner to the world. She currently perusing her bachelor's occupational therapy medical Degree from DY PATIL SCHOOL Of Occupational Therapy. And also works as a teacher in a tutorial.

I want to walk with ease on the sand,
Shoe digging struggles to find a piece of land,
I am alone and desperate to find a helping hand,
I wish my journey was about to complete as quick
as a spelling
wand,
God Pity on my eyes that are only able to sand
scan,
When I complete my incomplete I will stand,
I know people will barge in and argue if you strug-
gle why do
Do you walk on the sand?
I would dip into peace and lit a partial smile on my
face like the
first bloom of spring strand,
And speak
Is there a day without problems canned
But do we stop handling them or leave them to
abandon or
banned
Rather we walk on our problematic sand.
-Richa Dewani

SCHOOL,
Stepped in with crying faces thinking the whole
idea was cruel,
Then stopped remove the safety pin napkin to
clean the not so cute
drool,
You got used to everyday laughing talking studying to your friendship
fool,

From kids to teens got into stuff that thought to be cool,

Bunking, copying, enjoying were enough to fire the study fuel,

Fighting for the First bench to the journey to the backbench was a jewel,

Then being the school seniors kind of being the gang rule,

Being a teacher's favourite especially to get chalks and roam in corridors of

school,

Sticky oily hair back and uniform not so cool,

Tried hair and uniform tricks to look kind of hot but still remained fool,

Nerdy and not so nerdy all in a line for the annual fest and sporting pool,

Passed the school and still happily cried with the same drool,

Uniform hanging in my old wardrobe still over-rule,

And I have to admit I miss school,

I miss school!

-Richa Dewani

9-5 office chap,
Frustrated head wearing the smiling cap,
Want to sleep in my mother's lap,
Wanting own self to slap,
Thinking over all life decisions scrap,
But still got into a tensed and unappreciated flap,
Oh shit, then realized it's a trap,
Taking unpredictable desk naps,
being caught in action crap,
Money nor enough for life neither for travel map,
Standing in between of stress and unenthusiastic gap,
Need to breathe within a snap,
Gathering ethics and passion for my next living wrap,
Oh yes, I quit my job like a hap.
-Richa Dewani

Look at that Dark and handsome man,
Oh yuck, how dusky is that woman,
Hard work printed on Sweating man,
But be a little girlish you stinking woman,
harmless flirts suit that cool man,
Oh flirting such a slutty character woman,
Handling Workplace and house both such an
amazing man,
Workplace and house? What are you feeding your
children you
selfish woman,
Promotion! wow you deserve it, man,
Promotion! Aah, you are the one sleeping with the
boss woman,
Make a difference with what you say, man,
It's isn't MANly to brag woman.
-Richa Dewani

ISHITA SHARMA

My name is Ishita Sharma. I write poems, micro-tales and quotes. I am from Delhi. I am a first-year student. I started writing in class 10. And during the lockdown, I created a page on Instagram (imperfect__words). Whatever I feel I penned it down and give it a remake in the form of poems.

I know it hurts But it's too late to say. You know my worth When it's my last day.

I know it hurts But don't drop any flowers on my grave Because it's too late I cannot hold them anyways.

I know it hurts You miss my talks any my smell But its too late To find it again.

For you, I have recorded some voice messages Because I know you realize my worth but its too late. Have written some letter with my fragrance on it I know you miss it But anyhow it's just too late.

Thave planned everything for you and written your favourite recipe That's in my closet You'll miss my hand's taste But baby it's too late.

-Ishita

I could have asked you to stay But there was nothing else to say, Do you even shed a tear? Because this was something for real. You vanished just like a nightmare But I am feeling you right there, Over a year I have gone through too much But it was not that much. We had the smiles And the world says, "they are the ones" We dated for many years But something was so unclear. Have you shed a tear? Because my eyes are swollen and sore But don't have the strength to stay. I try too much With my heartbroken lay on the bed With my eyes wide open Thinking to reset. Now I don't want anyone's help Just want myself to cry Leave me all alone With only goodbyes.

GULNAR KOHLI

My heart feels like a solid rock, locked up in my imaginary feelings,

Feel my emotion, they are just like a waterfall flowing through my veins.

Water everywhere sinking deep, need a hand but hesitant to reach

I see the waves coming splashing crashing away my belief, my self esteem my confidence

The strong flow of water dressed in cosy arms of death pulling me closer,

Sinking deep into the darkness.

Then I found a ray of hope, an anchor

The anchor of my innermost self telling me to hold on for the flower beds awaiting on the other side

of thrones shrubs.

Feeling the rush of negativity, sinking deep

Then feeling the power of the roar of a lionesses

within you

Hold on to the anchor, roar out aloud to negativity

Heads up move forward

-       Gulnar Kohli

AASTHA S KHIVESARA

I AM AASTHA S KHIVESARA. I BEGAN WRITING POEMS SINCE MY SCHOOL DAYS. WRITING POEMS HAS GIVEN ME CONFIDENCE AND A WAY TO EXPRESS MY THOUGHTS IN A CREATIVE MANNER.

MY WORK – RISE IN LOVE – THE WATER IRIS (BOOK)

THE FOREST OF ENCHANTMENTS WRITTEN BY CHITRA BANERJEE DIVAKARUNI HAS GIVEN ME A DIFFERENT VISION OF LIFE.

"IT IS THE POSSIBILITY OF HAVING A DREAM COME TRUE THAT MAKES LIFE INTERESTING " BY PAULO COELHO HAS MOTIVATED ME TO CHASE MY DREAM.

THE DECLINING YEARS

When the waves rise high,
And tiny tears fall through the sky!
When the Season of love disappears,
And the declining years appear!

Let your Grey hair shine,
And the wrinkles are fine !
Just lay down with a smile,
But don't let your spirit die!

When you find yourself alone,
Cherish the memories you own !
Laugh, laugh at your nasty plays,
And think of your loved one

When you bloomed like a flower,
Don't deny to stand in winter!
The seasons of life are beautiful,
So what if you're left with pocketful?

Imagine your life after death,
And laugh harder at your grave !
Explore the wonders after a deep breath ,
And leave the world with a charming wave !

आने दो ना पापा

मैं भी सांस लेती हूँ पापा,

फिर क्यों मुझे पहले ही मार देते हो पापा।

पत्थर नही इंसान हु मैं,

फिर क्यों मुझसे प्यार नहीं करते हो पापा।

इतनी बड़ी भूल हुई क्या मुझसे,

जो द्वार ही बंद कर देते हो।

तरस गई हु आपकी ऊँगली पकड़ ने,

तरस गई हु माँ की लोरी सुनने के लिए।

आपकी हँसी में मेरी ख़ुशी है,

एक बार मुस्कुरा दो ना पापा।

इस धरती पर आने दो ना पापा,

देखनी हैं विधाता की कलाकारी।

इस भूमि पर आने दो ना पापा,

इसमें रंग दूँगी अपनी किलकारी।

भगवान ने दिया है मुझे सब कुछ,

बस प्यार न मिला आपका।

एक बार मुझे अपना लो ना पापा,

बेटा भी बन जाऊंगी मैं।

हर लड़ाई को जीत लुंगी मैं,

आग मैं जल कर भी जीऊगी मैं।

बस छू लेने दो इस धूल को,

वादा हैं नाम आपका रौशन करुँगी मैं।

VANSHIKA SINGH

I am Vanshika Singh from Uttrakhand. I am persuading my MBBS from Subharti medical college, Meerut. Writing has always been my hobby and this makes me feel more connected to people, their thoughts and moreover, it makes me understand a simple word in more detail because when I write my whole energy works in the process to understand the topic well.

Instagram id- @_thevannthought

I still remember...

Standing beside your grave
My body filled with full of regrets
Still remembering you standing by my side
But it always haunts me to think about what I did
to you?
I was your heart for whom you devoted your life
You remember everything
The way I walk
The way I talk
My likes and my dislikes
The first smile I had
And those tears from my eyes
You were always there to support
I still remember
The first Art competition I won
You were dancing like you were the star
I still remember
The first time I sang on the stage
The claps coming from you were as loud as the
whole crowd
I still remember
You were always been a part of my happy and sad
moments
But when it comes to me I failed
I failed showering you the actual love you deserve
I still remember
The way I talked to you
When you need emergency treatment
and I had those so called important meetings

scheduled
I still remember
The day I sent you there
You cried and denied a lot
But I didn't listen to you
I forgot , that you have always put my wishes first
But when comes my turn I failed
I didnt understand at that time
I sent you there alone
when you needed your daughter the most
I had many stupid reasons to give
I didn't understand
the way you felt depressed ,
Trapped in a single room
With no one to talk
I made a fake promise to visit you every sunday
But I failed
I failed in every single step when it comes to my
turn
I didnt realise it even after your death
But now when tables have actually turned

I understand everything you felt that time
Isn't it weird that when I realise you are not even
there to say sorry?
But actually, can my mistake be forgotten by just
saying sorry?
"I am sorry " maa for everything I did to you
For every wrong word i spoke to you
I am here to tell you
How I am feeling now
Experiencing the same feeling you experienced at
that time
    -Vanshika Singh

Trapped

Have you ever thought of escaping a situation.
We all do.
We all have faced many situations in our lives
from which we need to escape.
Most of you must be asked that
 hows your life going?
Many of us answers
it's complicated, it's okay
but none of us or many few of us answers its happy,
it's good.
Many of you must be feeling lonely.
Have you ever thought of what is loneliness??
We all have people around us ,
 but still we say we feel lonely.

It's just a matter of feeling comfortable with the people around us,
so that we can share what we are feeling.
The complication is another word
we all deal with almost everyday.
Have you ever thought of what does complications means?
Everyone of us have different defination.
Like most of us hate maths and find difficulty in dealing with mathematical problems
but at the same time, the same problem is solved by one of our freind easily.
So what this means?
We make the situation complicated or they are already complicated??
As i said everyone has their own definition.
Have you ever thought of what is right and what is wrong??
The thing which seems to be right for me might not be right for you.
The things which seems to be wrong to me might not be wrong for you.
Then what is actually right?
What is wrong?
If a particular situation is wrong then why we get tensed?
I mean if the situation is wrong then why to care about it?
It's very difficult to find answers to many questions.

But nothing is difficult at the same time.
It only depends on us
it only depends on how we think.
 It's all the game of our mind in which we are trapped.

-      Vanshika Singh

चलो आज एक नया प्रण लेते है

चलो आज एक नया प्रण लेते है
अपने शरीर के साथ मस्तिषक पर भी ध्यान देते है
कुछ बात सताए तो,
अपनो को बता कर मन को हल्का करते है
कोई अपना कुछ बताए तो,
धीरज के साथ उनकी सुनते है
अपने करीबी लोगो की मुस्कान के पीछे के
ग़म को जानने का एक नया प्रयास करते है

चलो आज एक नया प्रण लेते है
तनाव को मिल बाट कर दूर करते है
हसने- हसाने को अपनी दिन चरिया का हिस्सा बनाते है
मुस्कान को हर वाक्त श्रृंगार के स्वरूप पहनते है
दिल से सारी नकारात्मक चीजो को निकालते है
हर चीज़ में सकारात्मकता ढूंढ ने को अपनाते है

चलो आज एक नया प्रण लेते है
ना उम्मीद कभी छोड़ेगे
ना होसला कभी खायेंगे
ना अकेले किसी चीज़ से परेशान होएंगे
चिंता अकेलेपन का साथ छोड़ेंगे
ना किसी को दर्द पहुंचाएंगे
सही समय पर लोगो की सहायता कर
उन्हे जीवन का एक नया उद्देश्य दिखाएंगे
     - वंशिका सिंह

तलाश

में खुद से मिलने की तलाश में निकलता हूं
यू इस कदर कई रास्ते पर चला हूं
कभी अनजाने से राहो पर

कुछ अपनो से मिलकर उभरा हूं

तो कई रास्तों में

अपनो का ही साथ छोड़कर अकेला चला हूं

हर दफा खुद से झूठ बोलता निकला हूं

सब सही है ऐसा खुद को समझाता चला हूं

कई रास्ते अनजाने से नज़र आए है

यू तो पक्षी भी मानो कुछ सिखाए है

हर दफा खुद से टूटकर

खुद से जुड़ा हूं

और मजबूत हो गया हूं

इसी गलत फहमी में नजाने कितनी देर जिया हूं

कई बार अंधेरे रास्तों में

रोने के मन को मारकर आगे बढ़ा हूं

कहीं रो कर कमजोर ना साबित होजाऊ

इस डर से उन आंसूओं को आंखो में संभलकर चला हूं

में खुद से मिलने की तलाश में निकला हूं

 - वंशिका सिंह

SAYALI BHADARGE

I am an aspiring writer. Trying my hands on sha-yaries, poems, articles and quotes in the language Marathi, Hindi-Urdu and English. Working as an HR for the well-known organization, and having writeup pages/handles on Instagram, Facebook and some online platform.

Pen Name : Sayuri

Email ID : saybhadarge2@gmail.com

अभी तो आई है हसी लबों पे,

कर लेगा दर्द थोड़ासा इंतजार।

-सयुरी

गुरूर था हमें हमारी हर जीत पर,

मगर ये मोहब्बत ऐसे हरा गई के,

कमबख्त खुद से हारने के मजा ही आ गया।

-सयुरी

वह कहते है भरोसा करना गुनाह है,

जी फ़िर मंज़ूर है ये सलाखें हमे ताउम्र।

-सयुरी

ये जिंदगी बड़े खेल रचती है मुस्तखबीर,

कभी उसके साथ भी वक्त बिता लो,

शायद दो तीन पैंतरे सींख जाओ।

-सयुरी

यह गैरों से भरी महफ़िल सजती ही इसलिए है,

के किसी अपने का दीदार मिल सके।

-सयुरी

कटी नहीं है ज़िंदगी अब तक अठन्नी बराबर,

और ये तय तजुर्बा मांगते है रुपैय्ये का।

-सयुरी

SARITA PAL

I am 27-year-old. I am a Ph.D. Research Scholar. I am doing my Ph. D. in Education. I am a teacher, researcher, motivator, writer, poet, shayer . I have started to write poetry since 2016. I have most preferred to write in Hindi language. As per my perspective you are showing more emotion if you write in those languages in which you have command.

I am a blogger on wordpress. I have written 44 poems on my blog. 485 quotes on Yourquote app. In Future I want to write more poetry, quotes and also stories and novels.

I am not a professional writer. I'm just a writer who writes about their own feelings, emotion, motivation, love, hate, winning, losing, sadness, happiness, pain, desire etc. I thought what we feel already exists in the universe, that means what we express in our writing is also felt by someone at least one time in their life.

वो बात कहाँ

मेरी लिखावट में अब वो बात कहाँ ,

ढल जाये तेरी मुस्कराहट पर अब वो शाम कहाँ ,

जिस पल में जिंदगी ठहरना चाहे अब वो मुलाकात कहाँ ,

खोने के डर से पाने की ख़ुशी भूल जाऊ अब वो खोफ़ कहाँ ,

जिन होठों की हँसी देख आखे भीग जाये अब वो एहसास कहाँ ,

जिसे सुन के दिल सुकून से धड़के अब वो बाते कहाँ.

जरुरी तो नही

तू मुझको मुझ जैसा ही चाहे ये जरुरी तो नही ,

हर एहसास को शब्दों में जताये ये जरुरी तो नही ,

अपने हर गम हर ख़ुशी का हिस्सेदार बनाये ये जरुरी तो नही ,

तू मुझसे अपना सारा वक़्त साझा करे ये जरुरी तो नही ,

तू हर पल मेरा ही इंतजार करे ये जरुरी तो नही ,

तू मेरी याद में तड़पे ये जरुरी तो नही ,

मैंने जितना सोचा था मै तेरे लिए उतना जरुरी तो नही.

इंतजार कर लेती हूँ

भीड़ में भी तेरे साथ होने का एहसास कर लेती हूँ,

हर आहट पर मै बार बार पलट कर देख लेती हूँ,

जब भी हवाए तेजी से छु लेती है मेरी रूह को,

मै आज भी अपना आँचल जल्दी से ठीक कर लेती हूँ,

आसुओं को मै आज भी अपनी पलकों में ही झीप लेती हूँ,

अपनी मुस्कान में अपने हर गम समेट लेती हूँ,

मै तुझसे बिना शिकायत के हर रोज़ ख़त लिख देती हूँ,

तेरे जवाब न आने पर भी मै रोज़ एक नया इंतजार कर लेती हूँ,

मै युही रहा

बेपरवाह मै भागता रहा,

न जाने कौन सी मंजिल थी के मै भटकता रहा,

राह कोन सी चुनू बस इसी मै उलझा रहा,

दिन की तलाश में मै रत को कोशत्ता रहा ,

थी प्यास जिसकी आज मुझे वो कल कहकर टालता रहा ,

नई उम्मीद लिए मै हर रोज़ ,

जिंदगी के पन्ने युही पलटता रहा .

ANUMEHA RAO

A medical student and a writer too.
A girl with huge dreams who believes that "life is beautiful" yes "har pal ye zindagi khubsurat hai". She wants to fly high and give importance to every little thing that matters. By her poems and quotes she is trying to spread love and happiness everywhere.

वैदेही: मेरी कहानी

नौ महीने तेरी कोख में पली,
फिर आते ही इस दुनिया में,
क्यूं डराया मुझको मां,
नन्हीं सी जान थी मै,
क्या बिगाड़ा था किसी का मां,
टूट पड़े थे दरिंदे मुझ पर,
उबलते दूध में डालने,
पिता भी कुछ ना बोले,
तेरी ममता के सामने,
रो रो का बिलख रही थी,
फिर बचाया भगवान ने,
हुई बड़ी थोड़ी तो,
माना गया बोझ मुझे,
"हो जाती तू बांझ" कोसा गया है तुझे,
आखिर मै भी तो इंसान थी,
घर में आई मेहमान थी,
छे साल की हुई,
बाल विवाह कराने चली,
पढ़ने लिखने की उमर में,
मुझको विदा कर गई,
दहेज की आग में,
जल रही हूं रोज़ मैं,
क्या पाप किया है,
सोच रही हूं आज मैं,
क्यूं घोटा है गला तुमने,
सपनो का मेरे जीवन भर,
औरत तब तक अबला है,
जब तक वो एक नारी है,
बन जाए मां,

तो वो काली है,
लड़ जाती मेरे लिए,
तो ना देखती मै ये दिन,
तेरे भी सपने पूरे करती,
बेटी तेरी रात दिन,
ना बैठूंगी चुप मै अब,
लड़ूंगी अपनी गुड़िया के लिए,
सहा जो मैंने वो,
ना सहेगी मेरी परी,
गुरूर है वो मेरा,
बनेगी वो बहुत बड़ी
-अनु

ख़्वाब

दूर कहीं ख़्वाबों की नगरी से,
एक शोर सी आई है,
दिल बेचैन है,
उल्लास सी छाई है,
खोल दो पंख अपने,
भर लो एक लम्बी उड़ान,
हमारे हौसले को जंजीरे,
कब तक रोक पाई है,
दूर कहीं ख़्वाबों की नगरी से,
एक शोर सी आई है,
बना लो एक नई पहचान,
कब तक रहोगे एक आम इंसान,
तक़दीर के पन्ने नहीं,

हिम्मत की मुट्ठी लाई है,
दूर कहीं ख़्वाबों की नगरी से,
एक शोर सी आई है
-अनु

हिम्मत की मुट्ठी लाई है,
दूर कहीं ख़्वाबों की नगरी से,
एक शोर सी आई है
-अनु

कारनामें ज़िन्दगी के

ज़िन्दगी तुझसे तो रोज़ मिलती हूं,
कभी सुकून से भी मिला दे,
बरसो हो गए हसे हुए,
सुकून से चाय की चुस्की ही पीला दे,
एक रोज़ जो निकले थे,
बैठे ज़माना हो गया,
अब किनारे पर ले चल,
बहुत तेरा तड़पाना हो गया,
खामोश सी रहती है तू,
फिर भी इतना तूफान है तुझमें,
क्या गुनाह है मेरा?
जो हर खुशी कुर्बान है तुझपे,
एहमियत दी जो इतनी,
कभी कुछ ऐसा करिश्मा दिखा दे,
बहाए जो अश्क तुझपे,
उन्हीं को वापस लौटा दे,
इतना नाराज़ मत रह मुझसे,
इंसान थी मैं बेफिक्र,
हैरान हूं आज अपनी हालत पर,
चल पुराने हमसे ही मिला दे,
चैन से सोए ज़माना हो गया
मां की वो मीठी लोरी सुना दे,
इतना दर्द मत दे अब मुझे,
मै सहने के काबिल नहीं,
घुट रही हूं अकेले में,
मुझको गले से लगा ले
-अनु

मेरी हसी देखकर,
अपना दर्द भूल जाती है,
जिसकी दुआ हमेशा असर दिखाती है,
मुझ नाचीज़ को सोना बताती है,
मा ही तो हैं, जो बीना बोले सब समझ जाती हैं
-अनु

GITANJALI SINGH

Hi, I am Gitanjali Singh (Geet) , a science student.
I love to write in my free time and everything that life
has taught me this far. I am not a professional writer but
gave my small efforts to speak up in the purest form of
words i.e, shayaris and poems. I feel like the mistakes
once someone has done should not be committed by
others. That's why I write so that even if a single person
get inspired by my thoughts I'll accomplish my motive of
writing.

ज़िंदगी

ज़िंदगी ने बहुत कुछ दिखाया

कभी हंसाया तो कभी रुलाया

कुछ मुश्किलों ने दिल को बहुत डराया

पर मन था पक्का इसलिए डर को मैंने हरा पाया

मासूमियत थी तभी तो बेवजह हंसना सीखा था

पर उसको भी खो देने का एक वक्त आया

कुछ लोग थे जिन्होंने साथ छोड़ा

कुछ लोगों ने अभी तक है साथ निभाया

हंसते-हंसते कई रिश्ते बनाएं

दुख व्यक्त करने से मैंने रिश्तो को है गवाया

ऐ ज़िंदगी तूने बहुत कुछ है सिखाया!!

- गीत

नवरात्रे

आ गए नवरात्रे

अब तुम नौ दिन मां के आगे दिया जलाने जाओगे

पर असली सम्मान तो अपनी मां बेटी बहन पत्नी का आदर करके ही पाओगे

तुम रोज़ मां की प्रतिमा के पैर छूने जाओगे

पर असली आशीर्वाद तो अपनी मां से ही पाओगे

तुम मां से अपनी इच्छा ज़ाहिर करने जाओगे

पर अपनी ख्वाहिश पूरी अपनी बहन से ही पाओगे

तुमने जो नारी का सम्मान करना सीख लिया

तब अपने साथ एक निष्ठावान पत्नी और खुशहाल ज़िंदगी पाओगे

तुम जो मां को एक नेक इंसान लगे

तब अपनी गोद में एक प्यारी सी बेटी पाओगे

- गीत

व्यवहार

प्यार इतना करो कि
बदले में दोगुना पा सको
पर व्यवहार वैसा ही करो
जैसा खुद के साथ बर्दाश्त कर सको
- गीत

अपने-पराए

ज़िंदगी ने लोगों के कई रंग दिखाये हैं
अपने बाहर वालों से कहीं ज़्यादा पराए हैं
- गीत

उम्मीद

उम्मीद करोगे तो रोना पड़ेगा
बिना उम्मीद किए सब कुछ मिलता है यहां
 - गीत

दिल के रिश्ते

मतलबी दुनिया के अजब किस्से हैं,
दिल के रिश्तों ने ही किए दिल के हजारों हिस्से हैं।
 - गीत

ताला – चाबी

अगर आप किसी की ज़िंदगी में अपनी जगह न बना पाए तो निराश न होना,
समझ लीजिए कि उनका दिन वो "ताला" था जिसकी "चाबी" आप नहीं थे।
आखिर हर ताले की एक ही चाबी होती है।
- गीत

मोहब्बत

कि मोहब्बत में लोग ज़िंदगी जीने की एक वजह दे जाते हैं,
खुदका ख्याल रखने का एक कारण बन जाते हैं।
जिन्हे दुनिया में सबसे ज़्यादा चाहते हैं,
उन्हें ही दुनिया का सबसे खराब इंसान बता जाते हैं।

-गीत

ज़रूरत

चाँद को चमकने के लिए तारों की ज़रूरत नहीं जैसे
मुझे जीने के लिए आपकी ज़रूरत नहीं बिल्कुल वैसे
-गीत

सोच

मत सोचो कि तुमने क्या खोया या पाया है
जो पाया है उसकी कदर में कमी करना मत
जो खोया है उसका बोझ कभी ढोना मत
- गीत

दफ़न

देह के बिना कफ़न में दफना दी गई हूं

मैं इतनी बुरी नहीं थी जितनी बना दी गई हूं

  - गीत

माफ़ी

माफ़ कर देने जैसा दिलदार काम तो बड़े दिलवालों का है जनाब,

यहां कोई किसीको खुद के लिए माफ़ नहीं करता।

- गीत

वक़्त

वक़्त एक दिन ज़रूर दिखाता है,

यहां कौन सच्चा कौन झूठा है।

मैंने सच्चे दिल वालों को अकेला,

और गिरे हुए को लोगों से घिरा हुआ देखा है।

- गीत

पछतावा

काश उसके जीते जी भी लोग उससे उतना ही प्यार कर
लेते
जितना उसके इस दुनिया से जाने के बाद करने वाले हैं
तो ज़िंदगी कितनी खुशी से बीतती
क्यूंकि उससे नाराज़गी कुछ वक़्त की होगी
और उसके जाने के बाद पछतावा ज़िंदगी भर का
- गीत

Love

If you can misbehave with the person you said you loved so much and doesn't feel sorry for that

Then actually you never loved that person because true love never ends

- Geet

Judgemental

Judging me will waste approx. 5 mins of your life

Instead utilise them to work on your own flaws

- Geet

KONICA SHARMA

My name is Konica Sharma and I am a five year law student from Jodhpur, Rajasthan. I always loved to do dance and also I love to do new things and experience how they work and should work. I also love to read books and always have been in dream to write something, either on a paper or my own beloved diary. And also I do observe lots of thing. And express them through words. And people sometimes can relate that. And it motivates me to write more and I love that.

I live with my grandmother in Jodhpur, Rajasthan. And I enjoy spending time with her. But, yes! I have parents they live in Mumbai, Maharashtra. So, that's all clear that I really miss them a lot but also I spend as much as time with my grandmother.

I have always been introvert and that made me write things. But also at the same time I am extrovert with some. I have always been lucky to be around beautiful people. My whole life is wonderful and support at what I want to do. Most of the time you can find me with either babies or animals or doing something good for nature and yes obviously because I love animals and nature I am a vegan! And all the time I have thought to do something for our Mother Earth! For which I have an account on Instagram named as "@_iam_veganised_ " . My friends, and other vegan have also supported me. So, I thank them for everything!

So, yeah that's all with it. That's me!

Thanks for reading!

नैनों में बसते हो,
जब भी याद करते हैं।
प्यार आता है हमें,
जब भी तुम्हें देखते हैं।
हसीन होता है हरपाल तुम्हारे साथ,
हम तो तुम्हारे संग रहने को अक्सर बहाने ढूँढते हैं।
देखते हो जब आप मुझे प्यार से,
दीवाने हम तुम्हें देखकर घायल हो जाते हैं।
और कितना तड़पना है हमें,
बस हम तो आपके इंतेज़ार में सदियोंसे ना सोए है।

कर सकता है हासिल अपने मुक़ाम को,
पूरा करना है जो जिंदगी को,
कुछ नहीं हो सकता किसी सफलता के लिए तमन्ना से,
जब तक मुक़ाम हासिल करने के लिए प्रयास ना हो।

सच कहने से डरते है, इसीलिए झूट बोला जाता है,
पता है कोई काम सही नही है,
फिर भी वो करना पदता है,
यह पेट का मामला है साहब,
नही चाहो तो भी चोरी करना ही पड़ता है,
महनत करना चाहते है,
पर मौक़ा मिलता नहीं,
 बिना चोरी किए पेट भी भरता नहीं।

प्रिथ्वी ने दिया जो चाहिए था,
मैंने कुछ किया जो ज़रूरी था,
कितना कुछ बर्बाद किया हमने,
क्या किसिको ज़रा सा भी अंदाज़ा था?
मार्दिया हमने बेजुबानो को,
क्या उनका जीना का यही काम था?
सच बोले तो जीव जीव पर निर्भर है,
इसकी वजह से नजाने कितने
 बेजुबान कुर्बान हुए है।

MOHIT SAINI

Hey guys, this is Mohit Saini from Rajasthan. I am pursuing my Btech in computer science under RTU, Kota. I am writing from last two years.

Actually, I am an introvert type since childhood and this habit turned me into a writer. I like to be alone and enjoy my own company and this motivates me always to write. I always like to talk about spirituality, discovering myself, exploring and observing things around me. I normally express myself and my experiences through my writings.

Thank you Lapsus Creation for giving me this opportunity to letting me be a part of their anthology.

दो पल की ज़िन्दगी चार शब्द मेरी कहानी है,
दो शब्द मैं लिख चुका बाकी मेरी जवानी है!

ये आइना कुछ कहता है,
उस ओर जरूर कोई रहता है!

वो तस्वीर कुछ झूठी थी,
होठो पर हसी आँखे भीगी थी!

एक दोस्त मिला तो कहता है रोया कर
देर रात जगने पर कहता तू सोया कर,
मैं सोया करूँगा तेरे सामने रोया करूँगा
तू बस मेरी ख़ामोशी सुन लिया कर!

काश तुमने फर्ज़ ना कर अहसान किया होता,
ज़िम्मेदार बनने से कर्ज़दार बनना आसान है!

मेरा कल मैं भुला रहा, मेरा कल मुझे बुला रहा
मेरा कल कुछ थमा रहा, मेरा कल मैं गवा रहा!

ये आँशु झूठे भी तो हो सकते है ना
तुम ख़ुश होकर भी तो रो सकते हो ना,
रोता मैं भी हुँ पर आँशु छुपाता हुँ ना
दुखी होकर भी तो मुस्कुराता हुँ ना!
मैं निकल पड़ा उस रौशनी के एहसास में,
कई सितारे गवा दिए एक जुगनू की तलाश मे!

उसकी रूह को छूकर धड़कन को सुनना है,
हटा जुल्फों को उसके माथे को चूमना है!

जाते-जाते अपनी गुमनाम पहचान दे गया
ना होते हुए भी होने का अहसास दे गया,
दुखी नहीं हुँ मैं, पर तू मेरी खुशी ले गया
मैं जीना चाहता हुँ, पर तू वजह ले गया!

ये दौड़ता समय मैं सोता रहा
अपनों के बीच अकेला होता रहा,
ये हस्ते चेहरे मैं रोता रहा
इस भीड़ में खुद को खोता रहा!

ना मेरी ख़ुशी बड़ी ना छोटा तेरा गम,
इस अजनबी दुनिया में तू ही मेरा सनम!

बहुत कुछ लिखना चाहा पर आज लिख ना पाया,
शायद श्याही से ज़्यदा कागज पर पानी उतर आया!

मेरे दोस्त में कुछ चाय का एहसास है,
दिखने में काला, बातों में मिठास है!
मेरी ज़िन्दगी भले सस्ती रही
मैं मौत महंगी चाहता हुँ,
मेरे जन्म पर सिर्फ मैं रोया
मौत पर दुनिया रुलाना चाहता हुँ!

"काश ऐसा हो पाता"

आँख बंद करके मैं सब देख पाता
बिना कुछ बोले सब कुछ कह पाता,
काश ऐसा हो पाता

जो मैंने चाहा मेरा हो पाता
अपनों से बिछड़ने का वक़्त नहीं आता,
काश ऐसा हो पाता

गैरों की दुनिया में कोई अपना हो पाता
मैं इस भीड़ में अकेला ना होता,
काश ऐसा हो पाता

कोई अपना होता जो बिना बोले सब समझ पाता
जिसके गले लग मैं रो पाता,
काश ऐसा हो पाता!

"ख्वाब"

मानो एक हसीन ख्वाब टूटा था

मैंने हक़ीक़त में कदम रखा था,

मैं अपनी उम्र से बड़ा हुआ था

अपनों के बीच भी अकेला खड़ा था,

किसी ने ना मुझे देखा ना सुना था

सबने कुछ ना कुछ खोया था,

ना कुछ खाया ना मैं सोया था

उस रात मैं सिर्फ रोया था,

मैंने मेरा सबकुछ खोया था

मेरा कोई अपना चिता पर सोया था!

"वो लड़का"

उसने अब नखरे करने छोड़ दिए

उसे डर जिम्मेदारी का सता रहा,

जो खुद के लिए जिया करता

अपनों के लिए घंटो तक जाग रहा,

उसने सपने देखने छोड़ दिए

उसे साया कल का डरा रहा,

जो कभी रो दिया करता था

आज खुद को मजबूत बना रहा!

ANKUR VERMA

I'm Ankur Verma, 20 years old pursuing B-TECH Textile Engineering from Uttar Pradesh Textile Technology Institute (formerly known as GCTI , KANPUR) . I'm from faridabad , Haryana. Apart from my other hobbies, writing poetries is my favorite one . I love to write in my free time and that seems to be a very interesting part of life. It's not just my hobby but also that of what I think.

देखा पहली दफा उसे , तो मन घबराया था

हैं बस वो मेरी , एसा दिल ने बतलाया था

जताना इश्क आता नहीं, ये अगर तुमने समझा होता

यू कहानी अधूरी होती नहीं , हम बीच धागा अगर सुलझा होता

तुम नायाब हो ,

इश्क ए धागे मे बुना एक ख्वाब हो

मै कलम की स्याही तो ,

तुम लिखी पूरी मोहब्बत ए किताब हो

आई जब इश्क़-ए-महफ़िल में , तो तुम्हे देखता रहा में

ना बातें ना नजरे ए मुलाकात हुई , बस ये सोचता रहा में

की मनाया तो बहुत उसे , पर रूठा रहा वो

ये दिल हैं माना नहीं , टूटा रहा वो

जाना मन चाहता हैं सब खुशियाँ तुझ पे लूटा दू

तेरे हँसते चेहरे को और खिलखिला दू

यू तो अब शायद मुकम्मल ना हो तुझसे मिल पाना

तेरी तस्वीर देखे सारा दिन बिता दू

ये ढलता सूरज मेरी उदासी दिखा रहा हैं

दिखता चांद मेरी तन्हाई बता रहा हैं

और यू तो हर मुश्किल संभाल लेता हूँ मैं

तेरे बिना ये मन मुझे अधूरा सा बता रहा हैं

जब दिख जाओ कही तुम दिल थाम साथ हैं सोच लिया करता हूँ

अकेले में याद कर तुम्हे , पलकें भिगो लिया करता हू

मोहब्बत मेरी भी सच्ची थी ये जान लेना तुम हर आशिक का इश्क मुकम्मल
हो ऐसा जरुरी तो नही मान लिया करता हूँ

कुछ खुदा की मर्जी कुछ वक्त बेवक्त था

जाना तुम्हारा साथ मेरे बख्त मे ना था

सुना हैं मोहब्बत मे हर शक्स होता ताराज हैं

मैं ना हुआ इसमें मैं बदकिस्मत था

मुम्किकत ए इश्क की माशूका हैं वो ऐसा लगता हैं

तेरा मेरा साथ ना होना हर पल खलता हैं

सर-ए-बज़्म मे किया मुझे बदनाम उसने था

इश्क मे हूँ सोचा सब चलता हैं

एक रोज़ मेने भी इज़हार- ए- इश्क़ था किया

बात छुटी रात बीती ना उसने इंकार किया

शायद वो ख़फा हुई मुझसे थी

इसलिए ना बातें और बातों का ज़वाब दिया

टूटे दिल को समेट लफ्ज़ौ में पिरो रहा हूं मैं

तेरी यादों को निकाल फेंक रहा हूं मैं

यूं ना समझना नाराज हूं तुमसे तुम्हारी बातों से

बस बख्त को बदल खुद को बदल रहा हूं मैं

कुछ बीते कल के पल कुछ अधूरे ख्वाब लिखता हूं

मैं पन्नों पर अनकहे जज़्बात लिखता हूं

कभी फुरसत मिले तो उन्हें पढ़ना जरूर

मैं मेरे दिल के बिगड़े हालात लिखता हूं

मैं अपनी कहानी खुद लिख रहा

अच्छी या बुरी मैं सब लिख रहा

कितना मुश्किल होता होगा कभी जाना हैं

मैं जब अपनी ही मोहब्बत पर सवाल लिख रहा

आकाश वर्मा

नमस्कार...,

मैं आकाश वर्मा आशा,करता हूं की इस मुशकिल की घड़ी ठीक होंगे | मैं कोई बहोत बड़ा शायर या लेखक नही हूं.,बस कुछ दिल के जज़्बात,कुछ बाते और अपनी सोच लिखता हूं |और आशा करता हूं की आप सब को मेरे ये कोशीश पसंद आयेगी | (Lapsus Creations)बहोत शुकर गुजार हूं की उन्होने मुझे ये मोका दिया | मैं दिल्ली का रहने वाला हूं और अभी अभी मैने अपनी 12वी कक्षा पास कर आगे की पढाई शुरु की हैं | मुझे शास्तरी संगीत सुनना और सिखना बहोत पसंद हैं था मैं सिखता भी हूं |आशा करता हूं की आप सब मेरी ये कोशिश पसंद आये और लवज़,कलम,जज़्बात और हमारा ये रिषता लम्बा चले ...

धन्यवाद
मेरी सोच
आकाश वर्मा

ये रास्ता भैरूपीयों का था अकेले जाना नही था...,
किसी मुसाफिर को दिल देने तो दूर लगाना नही था...,
और वजहा थी की जाने से पहले हाथ पकड़ा था तेरा...
वहां जाने वाला हर शक्स मुद्दत से पहले आता नही था..

वो ज़रा सा चले ही थे और थक गए...,
हम भी ज़माने की तरहा उन्हे आज़माने में लग गए...,
और वो खामोशी से आगे क्या बड़े मंजील की ओर...
ना काबिले ज़माने के ये लोग उन्हे गिराने में लग गए...,

आँखो में दिखती हैं महोब्बत बस वो इज़हार नही करता...,

बे-मौके करता हैं मौके पर वो भी प्यार नही करता...,
कोशिश करता हैं की बातो के दरमियान कहानी हमारी आगे बड़े..,
करता तो बहोत हैं वो बातें कम्बखत मुद्दे की बात नही करता...,

ये कहानी अधूरी रहे तो अच्छा हैं..,
मैने हर किस्म का रिषता टूटते देखा हैं...,
देखी हैं सुबहा को रात में बदलती आँखे...,
कतरा-कतरा उस शक्स का बिखरते देखा हैं...,

मेरी सोच
आकाश वर्मा

ना होती तुम इतनी मगरूर ना हम थोड़े बे-ईमान होते...,
ना होती ये मुक्कमल दुरीयां दोनो में ना दोनो के ये अंजाम हैं...,
ना होता ये सिलसीला हमारे बीच ना प्यार में यूं नाकाम
होते...,
ना होती तुम्हे महोब्बत हमसे ना इश्क में फना सरे आम होते...,

ना हम किसी के हुए ना महोब्बत की गलियों में खो पाये...,
ना हमारे अपने,अपने रहे ना पराये अपने हो पाये...,
ना जाग करे ख्वाब सच ना आँखे मूंद सूकून से सो पाये...,
ना मांगी भीक तसल्ली की और ना ही तनहाई में रो पाये...,

मेरी सोच
आकाश वर्मा

उनकी उदासी हमसे अपनी खता पूछने आई...,
अपने गुनाहों की हमसे सज़ा पूछने आई...,
और हम आँखे तक मिला ना पाये उनसे...,
जब महोब्बत हमसे दिल का पता पूछने आई...,

ना छेड़ो मुझे यूं मैं मचल सकता हूं...,
लहजे से तुम्हारी तकदीर बदल सकता हूं...,
वैसे फकीर हूं मैं क्या ही कर सकता हूं...,
यूं वैसे मैं बूंद से सागर में बदल सकता हूं...,

जो जख्म से नही घबरते उन्हे खरोचो से डराओगे...,
किसी खंढर की तरहा तुम भी निस्तनामूद हो जाओगे...,
बड़े खुश हो रिषते तुमहारे मुक्कमल हैं अभी भी उनसे...,
मन भरने दो उनका तुम भी इस कहानी से निकाले जाओगे...,

दोनो मिलना चाहते हैं लेकिन दस्तूर नही बैठता...,
मिलना सब से होता हैं अमूमन वो साथ नही बैठता...,
कुछ इस कदर जता देता हैं वो नराज़गी...,
मैहफिल में बात हमसे करते हुए भी वो हमे नही देखता....,

मेरी सोच
आकाश वर्मा
कभी दरवाजे कुछ कहते हैं...,
कभी खिड़किया बाते करती हैं...,
वक़्त के साथ जो गुज़रे...,
अब हमसे उनकी यादे बाते करती हैं...,
दिवार के कान सब सूना हुआ दोहराते हैं...,
हर खुशी के पिछे छूपे किस्से...,
हर गम के पीछे की कहानी बताते हैं...,
किसी के आने पर सजा था जो कमरा...,
जाने के बाद उनके खामोश सा रहता हैं...,
ध्यान से सुना तो हर घर बहोत कुछ कहता हैं...,

मेरी सोच
आकाश वर्मा

WHO ARE WE?

Dreams are limitless and so is our vision. Being **India's 1st "Lead by Authors" Publication House**, Lapsus Creations connect your dreams with vision.

With our Guided Publishing approach, authors will have their own dedicated team of experts working alongside for their **BOOK** to come alive. We guide them from the very initial stage of their writing journey till, and after the book is successfully published. While keeping quality at the forefront, we understand the needs of a writer and work towards fulfilling them at zero extra cost.

Promoting creativity across the world is what we are determined about. While we work on the dreams of our authors, we alongside take care of their choices too.

With Lapsus Creations authors have the leverage to choose what they want for their dream book. We firmly believe in, **Of the Authors, By the Authors, For the Authors.**

Every dream has the right to get connected to its vision and Lapsus Creations has taken this initiative. Publishing every dream is our vision and hence we thrive on our motto **DREAM! VISION! LET'S CONNECT?**